MW01000989

Can Do Easy

TONY EY

Copyright © 2013 Tony Ey

All rights reserved.

ISBN-10: 1490589988

ISBN-13: 978-1490589985

DEDICATION

This book is dedicated to the young men who served in the eight teams of the Royal Australian Navy's 'Clearance Diving Team 3' (*RANCDT3*) in South Vietnam, who day after day, without a moment's hesitation, went into harm's way - not for Queen or country, or duty, but because that is what they were trained to do, that is what they had volunteered to do, and above all, that is what they wanted to do.

FOREWORD

It is a great privilege and pleasure to be asked to write a write a foreword to Tony Ey's memoir *'Clearance Diver'* and his novel *'Can Do Easy'*. Both works give the reader an inside look at the world of the Clearance Diver and a clear insight into the day to day life of Clearance Divers in Vietnam.

I had the great honour to serve in the Clearance Diving Branch of the RAN from 1955 to 1986 and have been and remain a staunch supporter of the Branch and the RAN Clearance Divers Association.

These books also provide great testament to the role the Clearance Diver has played in the Australian Defence Force, from humble beginnings as underwater workers, their role has become multi-faceted and incorporates much more than diving. Indeed diving, to quote a high ranking Clearance Diver, *"is just the way we get to work"*.

Tony's description of his career in *'the Branch'* could apply to countless other CDs who have had similar rewarding careers and will bring a smile of recognition to the face of many of his contemporaries.

I have served with Tony on a number of occasions, consider him a close friend and am quietly honoured to be the basis of one of his book, *'Can Do Easy'*, characters.

I recommend these works to you as definitive

descriptions of special forces personnel and especially the RAN Clearance Diver.

Edward *(Jake)* **Linton**

Commander BEM RAN Rtd.

Minewarfare and Clearance Diving Officer

Patron of the Clearance Divers Association.
Qualified on the 1st RAN Clearance Diving Course
in 1955.

PREFACE

This story is in part fiction, but it is based on numerous factual real life experiences of the Royal Australian Navy's Clearance Diving Team 3 (RANCDT3) which served in South Vietnam from 1967 to 1971 during the Vietnam War. The Team's official US designation was *'EOD Mobile Unit Pacific Team 35'* (EODMUPAC Team 35) as the unit was effectively under US command. It is the author's intention to provide in the following chapters, a broad-brush but quite accurate insight into what it was like to be a serving Australian Navy *'Clearance Diver'* in South Vietnam during the late '60s and early '70s. Although the actual official history of CDT3 may show many similarities to events penned on these pages, it was never the author's intent to provide a 100% accurate account of the bona fide record, but rather to create an entertaining and informative tale based on parts of that record. All the place names are actual locations. The names of individuals are fictitious but I have shaped the characters in this book around a mixed composite of the various men who actually served in the eight Clearance Diving Teams in Vietnam. I have done this because their distinctive personalities, their strong characters and calm temperaments were a very important component of who they were, what they did and why they did it. Their deep-rooted loyalty to both the Clearance Diving Branch and their mates, their professionalism, their mostly unconventional behavior, their ever present sense of humour and most importantly, their willingness, bordering on obsession, to confront life threatening danger head on, were all fundamental ingredients of what made these men stand out from the crowd.

In addition to receiving many individual awards for gallantry in Vietnam,

CDT3 was awarded:-

the **US Presidential Unit Citation**,

the **US Navy Unit Commendation** (*twice*) and

the **US Navy Meritorious Unit Commendation**.

*These are the three highest Unit awards
in the US Military.
CDT3 is the only foreign Unit to ever
be awarded all three.*

Other books by author:
'Clearance Diver – *The life and times of an Australian Navy Frogman.'*

CONTENTS

The 8th Team - Da Nang 1971 (author 2nd from left).

Channel Clearing - Hoi An 1971.

CHAPTER 1

It had been planned as a relatively straight forward mission, conducted at the request of the US Navy Coastal Surveillance Group based in Da Nang - the second largest city in South Vietnam. The patrol consisted of an ARVN protective force, (*Army of the Republic of Vietnam*) which was to provide security to a US Navy military advisor whose task on this operation was to plant a number of sophisticated acoustic sensors onto Cam Thanh Island, to the south east of Da Nang in the heart of Viet Cong territory. The sensors were literally microphones which listened for human conversation in places where non combatants shouldn't be.

Wireless signals from the implanted sensors would be picked up by reconnaissance aircraft flying in the area and that data would then be transmitted to *'Nakhon Phanom'* airbase, located to the NW of Da Nang on the Thai/Laos border, where it was collated, analyzed and passed back to the relevant authorities in Saigon for immediate action.

The four Royal Australian Navy Clearance Divers who were accompanying the mission had been requested to take part in the operation to provide Explosive Ordnance Disposal (EOD) support in the event that booby traps were encountered.

The group was inserted onto the island at first light by PBRs (*Patrol Boat River - a 31 foot fiberglass boat propelled by twin water jet propulsion with an extremely shallow draft suitable for riverine type operations*).

Within an hour of their insertion, the proverbial shit hit the fan.

Fully aware that they were in the heart of *'Charlie country'* (Charlie being the US nickname for the Viet Cong, or VC – Victor Charlie in the Phonetic alphabet), the patrol was moving quietly forward in single file along what appeared to be a disused track when all hell broke loose to their front. A solid burst of AK47 fire (*the Russian designed Avtomat Kalashnikov 7.62mm assault rifle – developed in 1947*) erupted from the jungle aimed at the forward section of the patrol.

Within seconds, the firing was interrupted by a violent explosion. The Vietnamese *'point men'* (forward scouts) and the Navy advisor who had been moving cautiously along the track behind the forward scouts, were suddenly engulfed in a blinding fireball which was immediately followed by a violent concussive blast and a rapidly expanding cloud of smoke and debris. The four Australian sailors and the remainder of the ARVN patrol had instinctively gone to ground when the firing had begun, about 30 meters to their front.

Their ears still numbed from the detonation,

the deathly silence which followed the explosion was at total odds with the thunderous concussion which had preceded it.

The silence unfortunately was very brief.

Then the very distinctive sound of AK47 assault rifles firing on full automatic began again, building to a barrage of rounds hammering down the trail towards the patrol's hastily acquired defensive positions. Fortunately for the Aussie Clearance Divers, the lead elements of the South Vietnamese Army patrol had taken the brunt of those opening moments of the Viet Cong ambush. In the brief seconds as Willy went to ground, he saw that his *'Chief'*; the Team's Chief Petty Officer, and Stan, their Petty Officer, had also found adequate cover. For the next few minutes, it was utter pandemonium as a torrent of automatic fire streamed in both directions up and down the track.

Then, just as abruptly as it had started, it stopped again – a deathlike calm engulfed the group.

Lying in the prone position behind a tree stump was Willy's best mate Pete.

"You OK mate?"

"FAAAARK!!!"

It was exactly the sort of response Willy expected from his ordinarily relaxed and laid-back mate. They glanced at each other with some apprehension as the Chief called out,

"Willy, Pete, you jokers OK?"

"We're right Chief." Willy answered.

Again, automatic fire erupted as the most

forward surviving South Vietnamese troops started withdrawing back along the trail at a rapid rate of knots towards the remainder of the patrol, dragging several wounded soldiers with them, trying to get the hell out of the contact zone as fast as their legs would carry them. Most of the withdrawing ARVN soldiers were firing their M16s to their rear on full auto as they ran, providing a brief pause in the VC fire.

As soon as the ARVN troops began moving back, the remaining South Vietnamese troops and all four sailors started firing selective short bursts from their M16s (*5.56mm semi-automatic/automatic standard service rifle of the Vietnam War*) towards the area they had seen tracer rounds streaming from just a few seconds earlier. When they had gone to ground during the initial seconds of the contact, the sailors had all spotted where the green tracer was coming from (*the communists had green tracer rounds while the US used red tracer – normally every fifth round in their magazines*) and as one they had immediately returned automatic fire.

After discharging a full magazine from his M16, Pete put down his rifle and brought his 40mm M79 grenade launcher to his shoulder, firing off several HE (*high explosive*) rounds in rapid succession.

Since arriving in Vietnam, Pete never went anywhere without an M79 grenade launcher slung across his back. The M79 fired a wide variety of 40mm rounds, including explosive, anti-personnel, smoke, fleshette, buckshot and illumination. The HE round had an effective range of 350 metres and contained enough high explosive to produce over 300 fragments with a lethal radius of around 5 meters. When used at close quarters, the fleshette round, loaded with 45 dart-like nails was particularly deadly. No wonder Pete loved the weapon.

During their pre embarkation training back in Australia, Pete had taken to this weapon with a passion and never missed an opportunity to sharpen his skills with the launcher. He was as accurate with the M79 as the rest of his mates were with their M16 rifles.

As the last of the ARVN soldiers dived into defensive positions adjacent to the Aussie Divers, they all stopped firing. There was no point in wasting ammunition.

"How many of the bastards do you think are up there?" Willy asked Pete.

Pete thought about it for a moment,

"At least a dozen I reckon. Did you see that Yank step on the bloody Booby trap?"

Before Willy could reply, they both heard faint moans coming from up the trail, and it definitely sounded like it was coming from a 'round-eye'.

"Shit, he's still alive."

As they listened in the eerie silence which followed, they again heard the groans which sounded very American.

Pete said in a quiet but very determined tone,

"Mate, we've got to go up and get his ass out of there before Charlie gets to him."

Willy was thinking to himself,

'Shit, we're Bomb Disposal and Navy to boot and this was supposed to be a milk run. What the fuck am I doing in the middle of this shitfight?'

Nevertheless, he heard himself reply to his mate, *"I'm with you Cobber."*

They both reloaded and slammed two full 30 round magazines taped back to back into their weapons as Pete raised his voice enough to be certain the Chief could hear him.

"Chief, we can hear that Yank. He's still alive. We're going up there to try and get him."

After a brief silence during which he weighed up the possibilities and whether the risk was justified, the Chief replied,

"Righto, we'll cover your ass as best we can. Stay off the trail, use fire and movement, watch out for more booby traps, and keep your fuckin' heads down. Charlie will be trying to get to him as well."

Willy looked across at Pete - the bastard was grinning. Willy vaguely remembered grinning back at him. Pete said as calmly as if they were going for a Sunday walk in the park,

"Ready mate? Let's do it." and then louder, *"We're out of here Chief."*

The Chief called out to the ARVN commander,

"Dai Uy (Vietnamese rank equivalent to Navy Lt.), *two of my people are going up to try to bring back that Navy advisor. We think he's still alive. We need some covering fire NOW."*

Stan and the Chief immediately started putting short but steady bursts into the scrub where they reckoned the VC to be located. The ARVN soldiers quickly followed suit.

Pete and Willy had just reached the closest cover, perhaps 10 meters up the trail, when the VC let go with several long bursts in their general direction.

Willy said to Pete after the firing had abruptly stopped again,

"By the sound of it I reckon there are only 3 or 4 of the buggers left. You might have got a few with that toy gun of yours."

"That's 3 or 4 too many of the fuckers in my book mate!" Pete replied.

From that point on, they had to move one at a time, leap-frogging each other as they went. This allowed them both to put down covering fire while the other one was up and moving. Pete was first. He took off like a scalded cat and dived for cover behind a solid clump of bamboo. Fortunately their ARVN friends had joined in with some withering covering fire from their 7.62mm M60 machine gun. This was their cue to get moving again. As long as the friendlies were firing, they had to keep moving forward.

They both stuck to good cover and moving only a couple of meters at a time soon spotted the American. He had been thrown well clear of the trail and as luck would have it, he appeared to be out of the Victor Charlie's line of fire. When Willy and Pete reached him, he was barely conscious and obviously going into deep shock from loss of blood. His camouflage fatigues were almost torn from his body and he was splashed with blood from head to foot. At least to his left foot. The poor bugger had lost his right leg from the shin down and the other leg was very badly lacerated. It looked as if a shark had been feeding on him. Willy said to Pete in a very low voice,

"Christ - cover our ass Mate while I'll try to stop the bleeding. Charlie isn't very far away."

Willy removed the American's own field dressing which was taped to his webbing and with strips of his torn trousers, did his best to stem the flow of blood.

He thought to himself, *'Thank Christ the shooting has stopped and we are out of Charlie's field of fire'*, then said to Pete,

"We've got to haul ass out of here pretty quick Mate or he's a goner. I'll carry him. Ready?"

"Roger that, let's go."

Without another word, Pete put down a steady burst of automatic fire to their front as Willy, as gently as possible under the circumstances, hoisted the US advisor onto his shoulder. The American groaned and mercifully lapsed back into unconsciousness as the two Aussies started back the way they had come as fast as their legs could carry them, zig zagging from cover to cover. As soon as the Chief and Stan heard their M16s open up, they both began to lay down some heavy automatic fire back up the track towards Charlie.

Once Willy started, he and Pete just kept going as they heard the reassuring sound of the ARVN M60 machine gun cutting loose again. That would definitely keep Charlie's head down for a while.

They kept inside the tree line and bolted for cover to the rear of where the Chief and Stan were holed up.

As soon as Willy had unloaded his casualty as gently as he could, an ARVN Medic appeared alongside him and immediately went to work on the American with morphine and field dressings. Stan yelled over to them,

"You blokes alright?"

"We're right Stan." Willy replied.

The Chief called over to them that the ARVN *Dai Uy* had requested an immediate Medevac (*medical evacuation helicopter - also known as a Dustoff*) for the American and the four ARVN casualties so the group had no choice but to stay put and hope Charlie didn't have too many more mates in the immediate area. He had also requested gunship support.

Pete and Willy moved into the best defensive positions they could find, sorted their remaining ammunition, reloaded and settled down for the wait.

Roughly 50 meters to the rear of their position, the trail opened out into a small clearing – more than large enough for a Huey (*the Bell UH-1*) to land. For the next 10 minutes, all was quiet. Charlie had either cleared off or was lying *'doggo'*. The patrol had no way of knowing which was the case and they were not in a position to try to ferret them out.

All they could do was maintain a defensive perimeter and bring in the Medevac helo to try to get the Yank and the wounded VN soldiers back to the nearest military hospital ASAP. They all knew the advisor was in deep shit if he did not receive serious medical attention very soon.

Willy's mind wandered – here they were on a shitty little island off the coast of South Vietnam and up to their asses in *'crocodiles'*.

A month ago none of them would have imagined that as four Royal Australian Navy Clearance Divers trained primarily in Diving and Explosive Ordnance Disposal, they would be in the middle of a firefight with the Viet Cong.

The six-man team had only arrived *'in country'* two weeks earlier. Their primary role was EOD support to the *'Free World Forces'* operating in Military Region One (*South Vietnam was split into 4 military regions – 1 being the northernmost and 4 the southernmost*). This operation was meant to be no more than be a routine sensor implant mission utilizing Aussie EOD support.

Cam Thanh Island was known to be a staging area for weapons and ammunitions smuggled down the coast aboard fishing boats to then be distributed to local elements of the VC on the nearby mainland. The head Honchos (*senior officers*) back in Da Nang wanted sensors implanted on various trails around the island to monitor the movement of the VC and their resupplies. They had expected the odd weapons cache to be found hence the Aussie sailors being requested to accompany the mission in case booby traps were encountered.

Willy was thinking; *'Thank Christ the Navy had the foresight to train us in combat infantry tactics before sending us up here. I'm also damn thankful to those infantry training sergeants back at the Army's Jungle Training Center in Canungra who in their own obnoxious way had prepared us for the worst'.*

Faintly at first, but growing steadily louder, they heard the comforting *'wocka wocka'* sound of an inbound Huey. Its distinctive thumping sound being generated by its two rotating flat wide rotor blades as they belted the hell out of their supporting cushion of air.

The ARVN commander had already established radio contact with the chopper so at the pilot's call, he threw a yellow smoke grenade to mark the patrol's position and guide the chopper into the rough LZ (*landing zone*) to their rear.

There hadn't been any incoming fire since Pete and Willy had made it back from their mad dash to recover the US advisor and all remained quiet until the Medevac chopper bled off airspeed and began its flare just prior to touchdown.

Then the shit hit the fan again. Charlie had been patiently biding his time and now let loose with a fusillade of automatic 7.62mm fire, all aimed at the chopper, which was starting to take some hits. Immediately the pilot cranked on the power and hauled on his collective as he side-slipped steeply towards the cover of some nearby tall trees.

He could see where the tracers were coming from and intended to get the hell out of the line of fire before his machine turned into a non-flying brick.

The Medevac pilot came up on the radio and advised that unless the troops on the ground could suppress the incoming fire immediately, he had no choice but to haul ass out of there. Everyone was aware that they weren't a big enough force to guarantee the safety of the chopper should he make another attempt.

The Huey pilot also passed on advice to the men on the ground that unfortunately there was no immediate gunship support available to them at that time. The ARVN commander called across to the Aussie Chief that it would be at least 15 minutes before any *'Snakes'* could arrive on scene to provide suppressing fire.

'Snakes' were the deadly AH-1 Huey Cobra gunships, armed to the teeth with a 7.62 mm, six-barreled minigun with a 4,000 rounds per minute rate of fire, an M129 40mm automatic belt-fed grenade launcher with a 400 rounds per minute rate of fire and M200 rocket launchers containing an array of nineteen 2.75 inch rockets tucked under each stubby wing.

It was clear that the Medevac wasn't going to get in until a couple of Snakes had either blown Charlie's shit away or had at least forced them to rapidly depart the area. There was no choice but to sit it out and wait.

As soon as the Dust-off chopper had safely cleared the area, Charlie decided he would probe their position again by fire. It was certain there weren't many of them out there but the little buggers weren't giving up. The Aussies had been trained not to waste ammunition unnecessarily although Pete popped off the odd 40mm HE round in their direction, just to let them know not to get too cocky. The ARVN troops were also playing the waiting game.

Once the Medevac had departed Pete said,

"Mate, if they don't get that poor bastard out of here pretty damn soon, his beer drinkin' days are well and truly over."

"Yeh mate, it's not looking good." replied Willy.

About 10 minutes later they heard the faint but distinctive sounds of inbound choppers steadily growing in intensity. There were two Snakes approaching with the Medevac helo trailing a few hundred meters behind.

The ARVN *'Dai Uy'* got to work on the radio giving the Snake pilots his estimate of bearings and distances to Charlie's position, relative to their position. At the call from the lead gunship, the *Dai Uy* heaved a red smoke grenade as far as he could up the track towards the ambush location and confirmed to the pilots an estimated bearing and distance from the smoke to the VC position.

The Snakes roared in over the top of the friendly troops on the ground, letting loose just forward of the red smoke. The firepower unleashed by these two helicopters was absolutely devastating, and close enough for the Divers to guess how Charlie would be faring. Both gunships were firing their miniguns and pairs of 2.75 inch high explosive and white phosphorus rockets.

The *'friendlies'* all kept their heads down until the gunships had each completed two passes. As they cautiously looked up at the smoke and debris to their front, Pete remarked

"Bloody hell!! – unbelievable - nothing could survive that shit."

Willy replied,

"Thank Christ they're on our side."

The Snake pilots came up on the radio and said they would continue to circle above their location until the wounded had been extracted by the Dust-off.

Within seconds, the Huey with a large Red Cross emblazoned on its nose and sides came skimming over the treetops, the pilot hauling its nose skyward to bleed off forward speed and flared smoothly onto the grass LZ to their rear.

Immediately several ARVN soldiers were up and running with the wounded. The remainder started to put down heavy suppressing fire in the general direction of Charlie but thankfully no return fire was coming their way.

As soon as the last of the casualties was aboard, the Medevac lifted off, lowered its nose, and rapidly gathering forward airspeed, thumped its way over the tree line heading for the coast and the nearest US hospital.

As soon as it was out of small arms range, the remaining troops all stopped firing their weapons. Apart from the sound of the circling Cobras, some semblance of peace and quiet had returned.

To their front, there was complete devastation.

Trees were stripped bare and their trunks left shredded and smoking. The strong smell of white phosphorus and spent explosive fumes hung in the air like a thick blanket.

The ARVN *Dai Uy* issued brief orders to his men and four soldiers scampered up the track to where the Huey Cobras had wreaked their devastation only minutes earlier, while the remainder waited in their defensive positions.

Inside five minutes the Vietnamese soldiers had returned, grinning and giving the thumbs up as they moved back through the Aussies' position carrying the remains of several VC packs and weapons. Clearly there were no VC left alive.

There was nothing left to do but get the hell out of there, and as quickly as possible.

The *Dai Uy* thanked the gunship pilots for their assistance and after completing two wide searching sweeps of the area, they set course to escort the Dust-off to the nearest medical facility.

The Chief gave the *Dai Uy* a thumbs up and the troops quickly formed up in a patrol formation with the ARVN taking the lead and the four Aussie sailors dropping back to the 'tail end charlie' position. There was about a two klick (*2 kilometer*) patrol back to the creek where the Navy PBR's were to extract them – from a different location to their insertion point due to the high risk of ambush.

The PBRs would be standing off the island waiting for the call to pick them up at their pre-arranged extraction point.

Firstly the patrol would secure the area and

then call in the boats. With some luck they would be back at base in time for a hot meal and a cold beer.

Four hours later, the Aussie divers were walking through the front door of their hooch back in Da Nang - dirty, disheveled and exhausted. The aftershocks of their experience were beginning to take their toll as the effects of the adrenaline had begun to wear off.

The OIC of the team, John Roberts, and Dusty Howard, the other two members of the team, were sitting in their dining area drinking coffee.

They both looked up at the returning crew with welcoming grins, very pleased to see them back. Their smiles quickly disappeared when they saw the looks on the four faces and the state of their gear. They looked like death warmed up.

"What the fuck happened to you blokes?" asked John.

No-one said anything. After a few moments the Chief answered quietly,

"We ran into a bit of trouble and the shit hit the fan."

"Righto Chief, before you go any further," John said, *"you all look like you could use a cold beer. Grab a seat. Dusty, what about grabbing the boys a cold beer."*

"Yeah a beer would go down pretty well about now. Thanks Dusty. Well Boss, the whole operation turned to fucking custard - big time." the Chief said as he slumped exhausted into a chair. As Dusty handed him a cold can of Victoria Bitter, he went on to explain in detail what had happened to the team on their first encounter with *'Victor Charlie'.*

A half an hour later, while the boys were

taking long hot showers, a call came in from the Jungle Surveillance Group informing John that the US Navy advisor had not survived the Medevac ride back to the Military hospital. He had died of shock and loss of blood.

They told John he had been within only 10 days of completing his 12 month tour of duty before returning home to the States. As Willy and Pete walked back in to the dining area, John told them of the bad news. It was as if someone had kicked them both in the guts.

All Pete could say was, *"Jesus Christ – the poor bastard!!"*

CHAPTER 2

Within a short time of enlisting in the Navy, Willy realized that the only thing he wanted to do was to become a Clearance Diver. These men were the Navy's elite. Their lineage stretched back to World War II where the forerunners of the diving branch were working in England defusing German bombs dropped on London during the *'Blitz'*.

Those men (all volunteers) risked their lives daily, going out to face the most sophisticated weapons the technologically superior Germans could produce.

The Germans were masters at manufacturing interdiction weapons - bombs which would not detonate on impact but would *'sleep'* for hours, maybe days, before their time delay mechanisms unleashed the devastating force of a 1000 pounds of high explosives.

Not only did those weapons have time delay clocks to deny the use of an area, they contained extremely sophisticated anti handling devices – in plain language, they were booby trapped with the intent of killing the technician attempting to defuse the bomb.

This was one of the most dangerous tasks expected of a serviceman during wartime.

A Minister in the Australian Government was later to sum up the role of Navy Frogmen when he said,

"To see danger and to face it calls for its own character of resolve. To seek to find danger in order to protect others, and to conduct that search in waters that shut out all sight, calls for a very unique character of human resolve."

It took enormous reserves of courage to work on those weapons of destruction day after day.

More than sixty years after that war finished, those brave men remain the most highly decorated men in the history of the Royal Australian Navy.

From this wartime role, the Clearance Diving Branch evolved into that of the Naval *'Frogman'*. Divers who retained the task of Bomb and Mine Disposal but progressed into areas such as advanced surface and underwater demolitions, sabotage, salvage, deep sea diving, ship attack and eventually into counter terrorism.

They were to become experts with explosives and weapons, able to approach a target by land, sea and from the air.

These were the men Willy wished to join and serve alongside. He knew it wasn't going to be an easy road as it was one of the toughest selection and training regimes in the military world. The failure rate had always hovered around the 80% mark.

There have been numerous books written about SAS (*Special Air Service*) and US Navy SEAL (*SEa Air Land*) training which provide some indication of what it takes to become a member of an elite force within the Military.

Vietnam was to be the testing ground for the modern day Clearance Diver. The government of the day decided they should not let the multi skills of these highly trained and versatile sailors go to waste.

Probably no smaller military unit in history has been assigned to a war zone. Six Clearance Divers in total made up an operational team with one Diver on standby back in Australia in case he was needed as a replacement. At any one time there was only one such six man team serving in the whole of Vietnam.

At the outbreak of hostilities in South Vietnam, The Clearance Diving branch consisted of a training establishment and two operational teams. One team was responsible for trials and evaluation of new equipment, general diving assistance to the Australian fleet and keeping its warships trained in the various methods of ship defense against swimmer attack, i.e. to respond to attack by enemy frogman intent on placing destructive explosive charges on a ship's hull.

The second team had the task of immediate response to any sub-sea problem confronting the Navy wherever it may be.

When the decision was taken by the Australian Government to commit a Clearance Diving Team to the conflict in South Vietnam, a third team, CDT3, was formed.

Prior to deploying, the first and subsequent teams

underwent intensive preparation for the war zone.

As part of their pre-deployment training, teams attended the Australian Army's five-day 'Staff Officer's Briefing' conducted at Woodside, South Australia. This included a comprehensive look at the history of Vietnam and an overview of strengths and activities of VC units in Phuoc Tuy province where the Australian Task Force was based. A limited introduction to Vietnamese customs and religions was provided, along with some very basic language lessons.

Intensive weapons training was conducted at the Naval Air Station in Nowra, NSW. Under supervision of navy gunnery Petty Officers, team members were given instruction in every firearm held in the Australian military inventory, including the 7.62mm M60 general purpose machine gun, the 7.62mm L1A1 self-loading rifle, the 5.56mm M16 rifle, the 40mm M79 grenade launcher, the F1 sub-machine gun and the 9mm Browning handgun. Team members learnt to field strip and maintain all weapons with their eyes closed. On the range, thousands of rounds were fired until everyone became extremely proficient in the use of all these weapons.

Training by the Clearance Diving EOD section included the use of M26 hand grenades, Claymore mines, *'Jumping Jack/Bouncing Betty'* anti-personnel mines, anti-vehicle mines, anti-tank mines, anti-personnel bomblets and foreign booby trap/improvised explosives device actuation systems.

The later contingents also completed the

Army's 3 week Battle Efficiency (BE) course conducted at the Jungle Training Centre (JTC) at Canungra in Southeast Queensland. This course became a pre-requisite for all Service personnel posted to service ashore in Vietnam. The course included patrolling, contact and ambush drill (fire and movement), harbour drills, ambushing, weapons handling and range practice, field navigation, camouflage, minefield layouts and clearing procedures, muscle toughening, obstacle and confidence courses, and forced marches.

Officers and senior sailors also completed the Army 'Code of Conduct' course at Woodside. Shrouded in secrecy, this course was designed to show Service personnel what they could expect if captured by an Asian Communist enemy.

They knew they were in for a tough time at Canungra. It was talked about far and wide as a particularly hard and demanding 3 weeks. Almost all personnel posted to Viet Nam had to complete the Battle Efficiency (BE) course at the Jungle Training Centre (JTC), as it was then known.

The team had heard a rumour that the US Military had sent some of its Special Forces instructors to do the course with a view to sending some of their troops over for training, but they had gone home saying it was too tough.

Situated in the middle of the hilliest country in Queensland, it was ideally suited for its purpose. It had near vertical mountainsides, tropical jungle, rivers, creeks, lots of mosquitoes and snakes and some very professional instructors. To a man they had all served at least one or two tours. It was very comforting to the team to know that these boys were not teaching just from a text book. They had been there and survived, and when they spoke, the divers listened.

There were about 90 soldiers on their course. Their day began with them getting roused out of their tents just before sunrise and it was straight into a nice little morning run, in typical Army fashion - neatly fallen in, keeping in step and wearing ruddy big clod-hopping Army boots. This was followed by a fast circuit through the muscle toughening course. After a quick shower and what was the Army's excuse for breakfast, it was straight into the day's sadistic training program. Numerous field classes were held so that they could go from the theory straight to the practical. Regular Infantry troops would give demonstrations prior to everyone practising the real thing.

In Canungra they didn't play games. While the group were practising the skills of Fire and Movement, the instructors were actually firing live ammunition just over their heads from an old water cooled .303 caliber Vickers machine gun. They were told it was to encourage them to keep their heads down. No-one needed much reminding after that.

A lot of time was spent patrolling and learning how to stay alive army style, day and night. On the occasional rare night that they were in the main camp, evening lectures were the norm with updated briefings direct from the war zone, VC tactics, map reading and a hundred other things that were designed to keep them alive.

When the team finally arrived in Viet Nam they were quite shocked to find how ignorant their Americans allies were about the country and the people they were sent to fight. Some US troops arrived in Viet Nam not even knowing where the hell to find the country on a map of the world.

The Aussies were certainly well prepared and it was a credit to the professionalism of both the Australian Navy and Army.

The group was split into 9 man sections with Willy and Matt (*Matt was destined to be the one who would remain behind as standby*) being paired in one section together.

Each section consisted of two men on 'point' carrying US M16s which had the capability of being easily flipped into full automatic mode, a handy function if you were the first to make contact with the enemy. One member carried the M60 machine gun with the remainder of the section carrying SLRs. As Willy and Matt were the fittest in their section, they naturally gravitated to sharing the 'Gun', day about. As it weighed about 30 pounds with a 100 round belt of ammunition, many of the soldiers did their best to avoid carrying the weapon. After a full day humping an M60 along with the rest of their kit, they came to appreciate a break as point man carrying the very light M16, even though the life expectancy of this forward position was not great.

Interestingly enough, the M16 was quite new to the Australian Army at that time and it turned out that the diver's intensive weapons training with the Navy had them one jump ahead of the

Army and the instructors of their sections asked them to run the training sessions for M16s once they realized the sailors proficiency with the weapon.

After two weeks of hell they were all given a day's leave in Surfer's Paradise. They were glad to see that civilization actually still existed.

The final week focused on applying their training to all-night ambushes and combined maneuvers. After many sleepless nights in the bush, the grand finale for the course was a forced march back to camp via 'Heart-break hill' with a live range shoot along the way.

On arrival back at camp they were all were put through the obstacle course for the last time. It was rumoured that one of the water pits on this course was regularly used by the Sergeants Mess as their latrine.

The Chief of the team best described the various phases of Canungra training in an article he later wrote for 'Navy News':-

"Weapons Handling:

This consists of learning the methods by which a soldier carries, strips, cleans, fires, cleans again and sleeps with the firearm which he has been issued with.

Contact and Ambush Drill (Fire and Movement):

What to do if one is confronted by the enemy. Contrary to general belief, one does not turn and run or shout some battle cry and charge headlong into the affray. Instead the well trained soldier carries out a precise drill designed to put him and his companions into the best tactical position from which he can engage and ultimately defeat the enemy. The drill consists of everyone shouting out what he thinks has happened, running in various directions and diving headlong into the ground which can be either soft bog grass, short hard grass, small sharp stones and gravel, large blunt rocks, a variety of tropical vegetation or mud and stagnant water.

Harbour Drills:

Any similarity between the harbour which sailors have grown accustomed to entering from time to time and the JTC harbour are purely coincidental. After having marched, doubled or stalked us through miles of South East Queensland, the Platoon Commander decided that the time for relaxation had arrived. He gave a sign akin to a flight deck officer telling a Chopper pilot to start his rotor turning. The platoon of some 30 men, breathed a sigh of relief and commenced a strange ritual which finally resulted in everyone laying down in a large circle facing out, weapon at the ready waiting for the enemy to arrive. The skill required for a Platoon Commander to select a suitable site for a harbour is immense. He must select an area some 50 yards in diameter, the terrain such that Platoon headquarters, the centre of the circle, must be on level ground, well grassed and preferably under a shady tree. The remainder of the circle around the circumference of which he places his platoon in pairs must be sloping so that when the soldier faces out, his head must be lower than his feet. The ground must be covered with small stones, large boulders or ant hills, and in the obvious course of streams of rain water. It is in this harbour that troops will remain for a short period or overnight. Should the stay be overnight, the soldiers' comfort is greatly improved as he is allowed to erect his HOOCHIE, which is a six foot square of moth eaten waterproof material which he strings between two trees about two feet from the ground. Beneath this he prepares his bed, consisting of another waterproof sheet on top of which is placed a sleeping bag, best described as two ultra-thin blankets covered by two almost sheer sheets of silk. All this clips together, blankets on the inside and into which the soldier crawls. Considering the amount of sleep the soldier in the field receives, I sometimes considered this to be over-complicated.

Ambushing:

This is the art of being strategically placed on the ground so as to trap an unsuspecting enemy. Once again the skill required and the thought that goes into the selection of the site is paramount. In practice, what happens is that a section is positioned on the ground, invariably at night, facing a track or road - weapons at the ready, and there you wait. You are not allowed to move, flinch, scratch, pass wind, cough or talk. This may sound easy. However consider the case of two sailors together in a mass of bushes for camouflage, the presence of flies, ants and a variety of bush animals, having marched halfway across Queensland, not had a decent meal for days to complicate matters further, not having been allowed the use of a latrine for hours. Eventually, when you least expect it, the enemy arrives. All Hell breaks loose, blank ammunition is expended in profusion all around you. You blink, allow yourself the luxury of a cough, a scratch and all the normal body functions you have been deprived of and then discover that you have forgotten to load your weapon, the enemy by now had disappeared and you had not fired a round.

Miscellaneous:

Under this heading we were taught such subjects as the Confidence course, best described as a dozen or so objects such as pools of stagnant water into which you jump, barbed wire to crawl under, mud, tunnels of wind and water to negotiate, slippery logs to walk across and a variety of obstacles crossed by ropes.

Muscle Toughening:

Designed to exercise those few muscles which the remainder of the course has not tortured.

Obstacle Course:

This is the conventional course we have all either experienced or known about.

We spent nine days of the course living in the bush. On these days one carried on his back all he could eat, wear, sleep in, on and under, drink etc.

The average day's food (24 hours) was:-

Breakfast: cup of instant coffee; one or two cereal blocks. These are best described as extremely tough.

Lunch: Cup of instant tea or coffee; a packet of biscuits (these are pre-broken and are completely devoid of taste and possess an odor akin to cardboard); a small tin of Kraft cheese.

Dinner: THIS IS THE MEAL OF THE DAY! Cup of instant tea or coffee; a selection of the following:-

Vienna Sausages - like valve rubber.

Luncheon meat.

Tuna in oil - use your imagination.

Sausages and veges - two 2 inch sausages, the remainder carrots.

Corned Beef ration - standard fare since World War One.

Added to this there were such things as curry powder, soup powder, instant rice (takes 10 minutes to cook), condensed milk, sugar, a 10c chocolate block, a packet of fruit drops (recently included for National Servicemen) and last but not least, six sheets of 4x4, polished one side, matte the other.

In conclusion, I feel that the main points to be learned from this course were:-

1. Do not join the Army.

2. If you do, do not become a foot soldier.

3. If you are thrown into battle, quickly become Platoon Commander, otherwise you will find survival difficult.

4. All the mountains in Australia are in the south-east of Queensland."

At Canungra the sailors were introduced to the *"Nine Rules"* covering Australian conduct whilst in Viet Nam.

They are worth repeating as they highlight traditional Aussie values, even though they may not have always been followed to the letter:-

1. *Remember we are here only to help; we make no demands and seek no special treatment.*

2. *Try to understand the people, their way of life; customs and laws.*

3. *Learn the simple greetings of the Vietnamese language and use them frequently.*

4. *Treat friendly people, particularly women with respect and courtesy.*

5. *Don't attract attention by rude behavior or larrikinism.*

6. *Avoid separating us from the Vietnamese by a display of great wealth or privilege.*

7. *Make friends among the soldiers and people of Viet Nam.*

8. *Remember decency and honesty are the signs of a man and a soldier; bad manners are the sign of a fool.*

9. *Above all remember you are an Australian, by your actions our country is judged. Set an example of sincerity and fair play in all your dealings with Vietnamese and with other people who are assisting them.*

CHAPTER 3

Clearance Diving Team 3 (*CDT3*) was to be located, as part of the Australian commitment to the war effort, in 3 Corps (*Military Region 3*). Primarily they would be responsible for locating and dealing with any mine threat to the inbound cargo and troop vessels at anchor in Vung Tau harbour, prior to the ships moving upstream to unload their precious cargoes in the port of Saigon. Secondly they were seconded to the US Military to be used for Explosive Ordnance Disposal tasks both above and below the high water mark.

As the US Military Command began to see the versatility of these sailors from '*down under*', they began to expand their tasking.

The first seven teams were to remain based at Vung Tau, to the southeast of Saigon (in 3 Corps/Military Region 3) where CDT3 was integrated into the US Navy Inshore Undersea Warfare Group One (IUWG-1) and the teams were involved in a number of major US operations including:

Stable Door- patrols and surveillance operations as directed in order to protect friendly shipping and military vessels from attack by enemy sneak craft, swimmers, sabotage and other threats.

Market Time- the blockade of the Vietnamese coast designed to prevent the resupply of Communist forces in South Vietnam by sea, and

Game Warden– assistance to the Government of Vietnam in denying the enemy use of the major rivers of the Delta and Rung Sat Special Zone.

Towards the end of the Australian military involvement in Vietnam, it was decided in 1970 to relocate CDT3 to the northern city of Da Nang in 1 Corps (*Military Region 1*). Here they were to operate totally independent of Australian day-to-day control.

And so Willy's Team found themselves operating out of Da Nang, the second largest city in South Vietnam.

The previous teams had operated in areas such as the 'Rung Sat Special Zone' (*Forest of Assassins*) and the Delta region of South Vietnam, operating from Swift boats (*PCF Patrol Craft Fast: a 51 foot, 35 ton vessel capable of 32 knots*) and helicopters.

The operating conditions changed for the team with the move to the north. Instead of swampy and brown water type operations, they found themselves on call to assist in the protection of shipping, particularly shipping carrying ordnance and explosives into the country through the main ports of Da Nang and to the south, Chu Lai.

They were also on call to respond to requests for assistance from the De-Militarised Zone all the way south to the boundary with 2 Corps and from the coast westward to the border of Laos.

CHAPTER 4

The OIC of the Team was Lieutenant John Roberts. John had progressed through the ranks to the senior enlisted grade of Chief Petty Officer Clearance Diver before deciding to leave the *'Lower Deck'* to become an officer. He was a country boy who had a steely resolve towards everything he tackled in his life. Tall and lean in stature, but rock-solid in nature, there was a quiet determination in John that was unstoppable once started. Respected by all his Team, he was the ideal choice to lead this team of highly trained sailors.

Harry Bradshaw was the Chief and he and John had known each other since they were both young Able Seamen Clearance Divers back in the late '50s. They were close friends who had the utmost respect for each other's abilities as both divers and leaders of men. Both had served over 15 years in the Navy. Harry was a quiet professional who simply led by example. The sailors looked up to him with the greatest respect and loyalty. He was their friend but they never forgot that he was *'the Chief'*, and so when he said *"jump"*, they jumped.

The other senior sailor was Petty Officer Stan Peterson. A hard assed Navy diver of the old school with a dry but sharp sense of humour. He was well liked by all and his attitude was *"If I can do it, you bloody well better be able to do it as well"*. He generally had a smile on his face but when angered had a well earned reputation for being a good man to have around in a punch-up. As a consequence most people preferred to stay on his good side. Stan had over 12 years service behind him and was expecting his promotion to Chief Petty Officer at any time. He was known to all as *'Stan the Man'*.

And so the remaining three Able Seamen were very much at ease with the hierarchy and command structure of their Team.

Able Seaman (AB) Willy Hensche was known amongst his peers to be a level headed and switched on individual who took every aspect of his job very seriously. With 5 years in the CD branch, he was the more senior of the young sailors and was considered more or less to be the Leading Hand of the Team. Like most Navy men, he loved a cold beer on a hot day and fancied himself with the ladies.

AB Pete Maxwell was Willy's best mate. They had previously served together in another diving team and were pretty much inseparable when ashore drinking and chasing members of the female sex. Pete was a tall lean slow talking Queenslander who had a reputation for sticking by his mates through thick and thin. He was like the rock of Gibraltar. The sort of bloke all mothers loved and wanted their daughters to marry.

On first meeting the third AB of the team, Dusty Howard, most would think he was the exact opposite to Pete. Fast talking, well tanned, hard drinking and always trying to chat up the girls wherever and whenever he could. Always looking for a good time, Dusty lived life at a hundred miles an hour and didn't take the world very seriously when ashore. On the job however, Dusty was just as serious as any of his mates.

All three junior sailors each had a minimum of four years in the CD branch so it was a very experienced and professional team of Navy divers who boarded that late night Qantas flight out of Sydney bound for the war in South Vietnam.

After a light meal and a few beers they all settled down, trying to grab a few winks before the scheduled fuel stop in Darwin. From there, another few hours in the air before they touched down in Singapore for a breakfast layover.

The five sailors and one officer arrived in Saigon from Australia aboard a chartered Qantas Boeing 707, having no real idea of what to expect. Numerous Army intelligence personnel had briefed them during their pre-deployment training but until the Divers actually set foot in Vietnam, it still remained an unknown quantity.

During the descent into Saigon's *Tan Son Nhat* airport, Willy took in the sights unfolding below. He observed to himself that the countryside looked very peaceful, very pretty and very green. Only the aircraft's unusually steep angle of descent suggested that this was no ordinary approach and no ordinary airport. As they neared the outskirts of Saigon he could see helicopters through the haze scooting low across the countryside in all directions, like bees searching out the sweetest nectar.

The Qantas captain thumped the big jet down hard on runway 25R and immediately went to full reverse thrust and stood on the brakes. As the aircraft exited the runway it became very clear this was not the normal run of the mill airport and Willy had the distinct feeling that their pilot was not keen to hang about on the ground any longer than necessary. Rushing past his small window, one after the other, were single Quonset hut shaped aircraft shelters. Some were empty and some were sheltering their charges – an assortment of US Air Force and US Marine front line jet fighters.

The taxiways were crowded with every size, shape and type of military aircraft imaginable, all heading for or coming from the two parallel runways – from single and twin engine Cessna's through to F4 Phantom fighter/bombers and lumbering four engine C-130 Hercules transports. Every square metre of the airport seemed to have some sort of aircraft parked on it. And there were choppers everywhere, many with their rotor blades either turning up or winding down to a stop. Willy had never seen a place with such a sense of urgency about it. He had been told before leaving home that it was the busiest airport in the world, and he now had little reason to doubt it.

Arrival formalities were relatively straight forward. A US Navy EOD Senior Chief was there to meet the Team and walked them through the official arrival procedures. Once they picked up their bags, it was into a waiting mini-bus and out into the sweltering heat and hustle and bustle that was Saigon.

People everywhere, all going about their business - war or no war. Bicycles by the thousands. Ancient little French Renault and Peugeot taxis and big lumbering US Military 6 wheel drive trucks pushing their way through this endless maze of people and traffic. Horns beeping, groups of schoolgirls bustling along in their immaculate snow white *'Ao Dais'* - the beautiful national dress of Vietnam. Armed white-shirted civilian police attempting to keep some semblance of order at each intersection but no one seeming to take any notice of their gesturing or whistle blowing. The windows of the EOD bus covered with wire mesh to prevent grenades being thrown through the windows. Familiar smells of Asia mixed with the pungent and ever present odor of Nuoc Mam (*the fermented fish sauce so loved by the Vietnamese*). This was Saigon, South Vietnam, 1970. They were in the *'Pearl of the Orient'*.

"Welcome to Vietnam Mates." said the US Chief.

"Thanks Senior Chief," replied John, *"where are you taking us?"*

"Well, you boys are staying with us tonight before we put you on a C-130 to Da Nang tomorrow afternoon. We'll get you all kitted up at our hooch and then show you around the nightspots of Saigon before you head north. Our villa is in Cholon, the old Chinese quarter of Saigon. My boys are the US Navy's Saigon based EOD Team and we've got lots of beer on ice and the ladies are awaitin' to meet you boys."

Pete piped up with his usual big shit grin,

"We're ready when you are Senior Chief."

"Yeah, I thought you might be," the American Chief grinned, *"we know all about you good ole boys from 'down under' and your beer drinkin' expertise."*

Their *'hooch'* turned out to be a magnificent old four story French villa. Some of its colonial charm had been lost due to an ugly eight-foot high fence, topped with barbed wire and broken glass, which surrounded the entire perimeter of the building.

Once inside, the Aussies were shown to their respective quarters. Willy was bunked in with Dusty and Pete in a large comfortable room containing six bunks with its own en-suite bathroom. John and the senior sailors had their own sleeping quarters. The sailors threw their bags onto the bunks and headed up to the rooftop bar to meet their Yankee allies and sink a much needed icy cold Budweiser. One beer quickly become half a dozen.

John, the Chief and Stan joined them and soon the bullshit was flowing as fast as the beer. Most of the US EOD sailors had been in country for up to 6 months and had worked with the Aussie Clearance Divers previously on several occasions.

It wasn't too long before the younger US EOD troops suggested the Aussie Divers should accompany them to downtown Saigon, and in particular, to the notorious Tu Do street, known far and wide for its girlie bars.

There were wall to wall bars, but what stuck in Willy's mind about Tu Do Street when he first saw it, was the large numbers of uniformed American servicemen spilling in and out of the bars and walking on the street.

Inside, the bars were crawling with very cute Vietnamese girls who resembled little China dolls with their long jet-black hair hanging down to their waists. They all looked 18 going on 30.

It didn't take long before the Aussie sailors had several young ladies trying to attach themselves to them with their standard approach, *"You very handsome GI, you buy me Saigon Tea."* The US sailors quickly told them about the *'Tea'*. Normally Coke or even cold tea sold at whiskey prices. The girls kept a share of the purchase price, probably around 50%, so it was definitely in their best interest to hustle for drinks.

When they discovered the sailors were *'Uc Dai Loi'* (Australians), the girls wrinkled their noses and gave them their first introduction to the infamous ditty sung by all Saigon bar-girls when referring to Australians:-

"Uc Dai Loi, cheap Charlie,
He no buy me Saigon tea,
Saigon tea cost many many Pi,
Uc Dai Loi, he cheap Charlie!!"

Willy smiled and said to Pete,
"Great, they've already heard about us so maybe they won't hassle us too much for drinks."

Dusty let down the side as the night wore on by buying a drink for just about every bar-girl who asked him.
"You're going to give Aussies a bad name you keep this

up Dusty." Pete said.

"Who gives a shit," replied Dusty with a grin, *"we're here for a good time, not a long time."*

The next morning, with bloodshot eyes and hangovers they couldn't climb over, the new team collected their kit issue from the Americans. Several sets of tropical camouflage fatigues, standard tropical fatigues, jungle boots, socks, K-bar knives, webbing, just about everything they would ever need. The American OIC told them that a full issue of weapons and diving gear was held by the team in Da Nang and they would just sign for them on arrival. He also advised that they were scheduled to catch a US Air Force C-130 shuttle to Da Nang later that afternoon.

After lunch, as the three sailors were packing their gear, the US Chief who had picked them up from the airport casually wandered into the room,

"No need to rush boys, y'all are staying another night. There's a bit of bad weather off the coast of Da Nang and all flights up that way are canceled until at least tomorrow morning, that is, if the weather abates. So it looks like another visit to Tu Do Street again tonight for y'all."

Dusty groaned, *"Ahh shit, I was looking forward to a nice quiet night."*

Pete piped up, *"Remember Dusty; 'good time, not a long time'."*

"Fuck off Pete." was Dusty's weary response, *"At least I'll get to see that little sweetheart 'Huong' again. She was a bit of all right. I think she loves me."*

Pete replied, *"Yeh, you and the rest of the fuckin' US*

Army."

The following morning came the news that the worst of the bad weather had passed out to sea and they would be on a flight departing Saigon at 1600 that afternoon. There were no complaints from any of the Team as it meant a few extra hours in the sack after another big night in the bars. Dusty was flat broke after an evening of trying to prove to all the girls of Tu Do street that not every *Uc Dai Loi* was a 'cheap charlie'.

The C-130 was crowded, uncomfortable and noisy. Web seats ran along each side of the aircraft with another two rows running up the centre. American servicemen in all types of uniforms and of all persuasions were crammed in with their kitbags and weapons.

It was cold, bumpy as hell, solid overcast and raining as the Hercules descended into Da Nang. The turbulence had the pilot working hard to keep the aircraft on track as he banked to line up for the final approach. Quite severe wind gusts were giving him a solid workout and the passengers some anxious moments.

As the chubby tyres of the Herc contacted the asphalt of the runway Willy felt a surge of excitement. After months of intensive training they had arrived in what was to be their own piece of the war zone.

They were all volunteers for service in Vietnam and they were about to put into practice what years of training had prepared them for, or so they thought. No-one in the team had served less than 4 years in the Navy. They were there because they wanted to be there and they had all been handpicked for the job.

As the aircraft taxied in towards the terminal, all Willy could see through the small window was low dark cloud, drizzling rain and pools of water lying about everywhere. While the four big turboprop engines slowly spooled down, Pete broke into a grin and said,

"Well boys; we're here - because we're fucking here."

That brought a smile to their faces. A typically deep and meaningful statement from the driest member of the team.

"You got anymore words of wisdom Pete, or is that it?" replied Stan with a smirk.

John cut in,

"C'mon fellas, let's round up our gear. Someone from the other team should be here to meet us."

The first thing they noticed as the ramp of the aircraft lowered and the port side forward door opened was the difference in temperature from Saigon. It was a hell of a lot colder. But that made sense; they were about 500 miles north of the capital and it was raining and blowing a gale.

Once inside the terminal it didn't take long to spot the grinning faces of Jacko and Shorty, two members of the team they were sent to relieve. While all were busy shaking hands, Jacko grinned,

"About time you bastards got here, we thought you were planning on spending your whole tour in Tu Do Street."

"We thought about it Jacko but Dusty hasn't got any money left and we had to get him away from all those

good looking sheilas before he started writing IOU's." laughed Stan.

Dusty came back with, *"Don't believe anything these mongrels tell you Jacko. They're full of shit."*

"Righto fellas, we can't stand here all night bullshitting" grinned Shorty as he turned towards John *"We've got a van outside Boss, so if you load up, we'll get going. There's a bit of a welcoming party organized for you blokes back at our hooch."*

"Christ, is that all anybody does in Vietnam – get on the piss." muttered the Chief.

"In your honour Chief." said Shorty with a grin.

Although it was well after dark, they were all eyes for the twenty minute drive to their new home. It was very obvious Da Nang was quite a different city to Saigon. Apart from the temperature change, it was much more spread out and far less congested. There were no cars, taxis, cyclos or people on the streets. In fact there was bugger all on the roads. It was like the place had been deserted.

Shorty was driving and obviously sensed what the new fellas were thinking.

"There's an after dark curfew in Da Nang. No troops are allowed on the streets in town and all the locals are tucked up for the night. You have to have a damn good reason to be on the streets after dark. We are one of the exceptions to the rule. Pretty well go where we like, when we like, which is a bit of a plus at times."

Jacko got back onto his favourite subject.

"We got the word you blokes had a pretty good time in Saigon."

"Yeah, good run Jacko, but a bit expensive, eh Dusty!" chuckled Stan.

Dusty continued looking out the window at the passing Vietnamese hooches,

"You bastards never let up. All I did was buy a couple of drinks for a few good lookin' honeys who happened to love me."

"If you bought me that much free piss, I'd probably love you as well Dusty." grinned Pete.

"Yeah, well just as well I've got good taste. I wouldn't buy you shit."

After crossing the Da Nang river, Shorty veered north and headed out onto what appeared to be a large peninsula. In the distance in front of them they could see the imposing outline of a quite sizeable mountain. Once again reading their thoughts, Shorty said,

"That's Monkey Mountain up ahead. We live at the base of it in a Naval compound called Camp Tien Sha. All the comforts of home. Cold VB, barbecued ribs and salad for us tonight."

Then with a huge grin, "A ceasefire has been arranged in your honour so we can get on the piss tonight."

The Chief grumbled "I thought there was a goddamn war on here."

Jacko laughed, "Plenty of time for that Chief. Tonight it's Aussie beer and American spare ribs."

The vehicle slowed as it entered what was obviously a military compound. An armed helmeted guard at the entrance saluted and waved them through. At the foot of the mountain they turned into a compound which housed several vehicles including two jeeps, a few 4x4 pickups and a trailered boat.

A sign on the front of a white washed single story building read 'NAVY EOD'.

"This is it fellas, we're home." said Shorty as he pulled up and honked the horn.

The other four members of the old team filed out the door with beers in their hands and it was handshakes and grins all round. They were all old mates of the new Team and they hadn't seen them for seven months. In a small tight community like theirs, everybody knows everybody.

Their first surprise as they entered their new home was the unexpected comfort. There was a fully equipped kitchen and dining area, a fully stocked bar, bunk accommodation for perhaps twenty, an office and separate sleeping quarters for the Boss and the Chief, a large workshop which doubled as a lounge with lockable storage space for personal weapons and a garage. The bar was hopping. Country and Western music was cranked up and at least a dozen US visitors in an assortment of uniforms were there to welcome them.

Bob Ryley, the outgoing CO called for a bit of quiet and said,

"On behalf of my team I'd like to welcome the new team to Da Nang. You can let your hair down a bit tonight lads as a couple of US Navy EOD types are in town and they are taking the weight for us tonight. Introduce yourselves to our American mates and once again, welcome to the sharp end. The tucker will be on in about an hour," then with a wide shit grin he said *"and*

we're not short, we're next."

So there they were; in what they thought was a war zone, drinking ice cold Aussie beer and shooting the shit like they were at a weekend BBQ back in suburban Sydney.

Willy remarked to Pete,
"Jesus, this is all right Mate. I can handle this. When's the war start?"

The next few weeks were to provide Willy with an answer that he certainly had not anticipated.

CHAPTER 5

During the first few days *'in country'*, the departing team showed the new boys around, introduced them to worthwhile and necessary contacts and briefed them in detail on the nature of the Team's roles. They happily signed over their complete weapons arsenal and gave them all their considerable ammunition and explosives inventory. They were keen to get home.

After a week, they were gone, departing Da Nang for Saigon and then home. Another week and the new team had its first operation with the Jungle Surveillance Group and its baptism of fire with the Viet Cong on Cam Thanh Island.

After having just come to terms with the events which had unfolded on that first operation, an urgent call came in on the radio from the Navy Harbour Security Centre. They advised that one of their patrol boats had spotted a small fire onboard an ammunition barge which had broken adrift from its moorings during some bad weather a few days earlier. The barge was loaded to the gunwales with 81mm mortar rounds, 105mm and 155mm howitzer rounds and 2.75 inch rockets. It also happened to be aground on a sandbar only 200 metres from the Da Nang harbour shoreline. The

Team was requested to respond immediately.

With 400 tons of high explosive ordnance onboard and a fire increasing in intensity by the minute, the scene did not auger well for the several hundred civilians living within a few hundred metres of the grounded barge. Stan, Dusty and Willy were on their way within minutes in the immediate response vehicle which was set up for emergencies such as this. With red light flashing and siren blaring, they headed for a pier they were as yet unfamiliar with to board the waiting Harbour Security high speed skimmer. After making several wrong turns, which probably delayed them by 3 or 4 minutes, they arrived at the wharf. The boat, with motor running, was ready to go. As the three loaded their gear aboard Willy looked across at the barge, perhaps 800 metres away. He could see what appeared to be a small but fierce fire shimmering on the upper deck.

Because of the close proximity of the village, they had no choice other than to proceed to the barge and attempt to extinguish the fire before the inevitable happened. Harbour Security had already loaded the boat with several items of firefighting equipment. The three divers all had their eyes on the barge as the boat was slipped from the wharf and the coxswain turned the boat away from the pier, easing the throttles fully open.

And it was at that very moment that the explosive cargo onboard the barge *'cooked off'* (detonated). It was the biggest explosion any of them had ever seen. The barge erupted in a massive fireball which resembled a small nuclear blast in both shape and intensity.

The coxswain didn't need to be told that there was no longer a need to hurry and immediately hauled back on the throttles as they watched a huge mushroom shaped cloud soar skyward. Throw-outs were going everywhere. Chunks of steel, mortar rounds and rockets were arcing through the sky in every direction, heading for the beach, and heading for them. They squatted on their haunches in the boat, now sitting still in the water, mesmerized by the incredible force of the explosion unfolding before their eyes.

For the next 30 or 40 seconds, near red-hot spinning metal fragments of all shapes and sizes, including what appeared to be intact pieces of large ordnance rained down over a huge radius surrounding the barge. Willy could hear the shrill whistle made by incoming shrapnel as it hurtled in their direction, some splashing down within several metres of the boat. It was crucial that they kept their eyes peeled for anything coming in their direction and hope like hell it would miss them. A number of quite large metal fragments were sailing over their heads and landing on the wharf area to their rear. Willy snapped his head around as he heard a loud crash and breaking glass close behind them. The front half of their truck had just been totally destroyed.

As the last of the debris splashed down into the bay, the huge pall of smoke that hung like a dark curtain in the sky drifted slowly downwind from the blast site. All that remained of the ammunition barge was what appeared to be a small part of the stern and what was left of what was most probably the wheelhouse structure and that was twisted and distorted beyond recognition.

There was silence in the boat as they waited for the last of the throwout material to come back to earth. The US Navy coxswain was the first to break the relative stillness, and all he could manage was a subdued,

"Goddamn!"

Small fires were breaking out amongst some of the nearer villages along the harbour shoreline. Stan immediately dialed in the Navy Ops centre frequency, which was also the frequency monitored by their team back at the hooch, on the boat's PRC-25 radio (*commonly called a Prick 25*).

"Cliffside, this is Mobile Bravo. The grounded ammunition barge has just been totally destroyed by explosive detonation. I repeat, totally destroyed. Bravo is proceeding to investigate extent of throw-outs and risk from unexploded ordnance. Please advise Harbour Security and any available EOD units to secure shoreline adjacent to Barge location. Appear to be numerous munition throw-outs and risk to civilian population from ordnance will be extreme. Presume high casualty rate in adjacent village. Suggest mobilising medical assets. Will keep advised - break - Mobile Alpha, this is Mobile Bravo, did you copy. We're going to need some help on this one Boss, over."

John came straight up on the net,

"Copied Bravo, we're on our way. You check out the barge area and we're on our way to the beach. Stay on this frequency. Mobile Alpha out."

Stan turned to the coxswain,

"Righto mate, let's head out there slow time and take a look. Take it very steady. We don't want to rip the ass out of your boat."

As the boat idled slowly out towards the wreck, they could see that only part of the stern remained, and that was opened up like a huge sardine can. Twisted lengths of jagged steel pointed in all directions like grotesque tentacles of some bizarre man made sculptured metal octopus.

Sharp deformed sections of steel protruded from the water for hundreds of metres around the wreck. Fragments of the hull and ordnance were scattered along the sandy shoreline. It looked like a junkyard; a very dangerous junkyard.

"Going to be a big job to clean this fucker up boys. There's shit everywhere." said Stan as he took in the extent of the throw-outs.

Dusty said to no one in particular,

"Thank Christ we weren't on the bastard when she cooked off eh? Never seen a bang like that before."

The boat coxswain circled the remains of the wreck at a distance of 100 metres or so, not willing to take his boat in too close. As Willy took in the extent of the damage resulting from the massive blast, it dawned on him that if they hadn't taken a few wrong turns on their way to the wharf, they would have been onboard the barge as it cooked off.

There would have been no trace left of them.

The blast had shredded the steel hull into thousands of pieces of all shapes and sizes ranging from a few kilos to the size of a small car. At least 90% of the hull had completely disappeared. Only 3 metres or so of the stern remained and that was twisted and mangled beyond recognition.

Along the shoreline they could see the beach was littered with mortars, howitzer rounds, and rockets, many still clustered together in their shattered pallets.

Over the following few days, the Team conducted its own survey to determine the location and condition of the bulk of the ordnance that had been thrown out from the barge. They found an almost intact pallet of 81mm mortars had landed about 2 metres from a Vietnamese hooch which had the entire family inside. Grandparents, Mum, Dad and 5 kids. Incredibly nobody was hurt.

The divers now had to get a feel for the scope of the cleanup operation. Their responsibility would be for the harbour area below the high water mark.

For the following three or four months the team was to spend the majority of its spare time recovering and disposing of the thrown out ordnance. Responsibility above the high water mark fell to the US Army EOD team which was based in downtown Da Nang. On completion of the cleanup operation several months later, their final estimate was that approximately 200 tons of ordnance from the barge had in fact not detonated, but been thrown over a large part of Da Nang harbour.

The team was later advised by the Vietnamese

authorities that two young men from a nearby village had been reported as missing. After further investigation by the local police it was revealed they were both suspected VC sympathizers and they had not been seen since the morning of the blast. It was a distinct possibility that these guys had sabotaged the barge and then either discretely disappeared or may even have been on the barge when it blew.

Remains of Ammunition barge which
'cooked off' in DaNang harbour.

Only about 10% of the hull remained.

CHAPTER 6

The Team had inherited a *'Mamasan'* from the outgoing team. She was a Vietnamese lady of indeterminable age who kept the hooch in some semblance of order and cleanliness and did most of their washing and some cooking. With the exception of Stan, the Team really enjoyed her meals. Stan hated the smell of Nuoc Mam and when she was cooking, he would leave the hooch with the parting comment,

"Don't know how you blokes can eat that shit!!"

(*Nuoc Mam is an amber-colored liquid extracted from the fermentation of fish with water and sea salt. It is a staple ingredient in numerous cuisines throughout Southeast Asia and features heavily in all Vietnamese cooking. In addition to being added to dishes during and after the cooking process, Nuoc Mam is also used as a base for a dipping condiment that is prepared in many different ways. Vietnamese fish sauce is usually used in moderation because of its very intense flavour*).

Mamasan lived only a few miles from Camp Tien Sha and she worked in their hooch every day except Sundays. Not a lot was known about her as she spoke no English, which was just as well, considering Stan's comments about her cooking.

Dusty discovered that her husband and only

son were away in the Military and she hadn't seen either for a year or two. On which side they fought, the team had no idea.

The Team had also inherited a mongrel dog and a small female monkey. They hated the sight of each other so the monkey, named *'Fred'* by the previous team, was kept on a long lead in the backyard, and *'Dog'* had the run of the hooch. He was a great watchdog and looked very much like a 'Queensland Blue Heeler'- a popular Queensland breed of dog back in Australia.

Camp Tien Sha was a US Navy installation responsible for supporting all shore based Naval operations in Military Region One and in particular Swift Boat and PBR repair facilities in Da Nang harbour.

The Australian team was on call 24 hours a day and their tasking was co-ordinated through the Operations Centre with whom they were in constant radio contact. There was a chopper pad only a few hundred metres down the road from the hooch so the team's ability to respond to calls was almost immediate.

The Aussies were not the only EOD team in I Corps. The US Marine and Air Force teams were responsible for Da Nang airfield, an Army EOD team looked after Da Nang city and the Aussies pretty much had responsibility for the rest of the Military region up to the De Militarized Zone (DMZ) bordering North Vietnam.

The old team had left them with a large collection of weapons that weren't all recorded on the US inventory. Apart from their standard issue M16s, M79s, pump action 12 gauge shotguns and Colt .45 handguns, they had a large selection of captured Chi-com (*Chinese communist*) and Soviet weapons, the most well known being the Kalashnikov 7.62mm AK47 assault rifle.

There were a couple of jeeps, two four-wheel drive trucks, a pickup and a 13 foot fiberglass skimmer boat with an 85 hp Johnson outboard motor.

Transportation was to be the least of the Team's problems.

They didn't waste any time in visiting a local disused quarry on a regular basis to sharpen their shooting skills with the large inventory of weapons they had inherited from the previous team.

Everyone had their preferred weapons, in addition to the .45 Colt they all carried as a personal sidearm. Pete never went anywhere without his much loved M79 40mm grenade launcher, Dusty liked the 12 gauge pump action shotgun while the Boss always carried a small pencil flare gun along with his Colt .45 and M16. John's logic was that if he fired a flare gun at short range into someone's mid-section, the bloke would be distracted sufficiently long enough for John to sort him out. The Chief, Stan and Willy liked the Car 15, a cut down version of the M16.

CHAPTER 7

After the excitement of the barge episode, they thought things might slow down a bit. John decided it was a good time to send Stan south to Vung Tau in 3 Corps to make contact with the Australian Army REMFs (*rear echelon mutha-fuckers*). It always paid to be on good terms with the Army stores types.

Stan didn't want to mess around with normal US *'milk-run'* flights to Saigon and then have to organize an onward flight to Vung Tau so he negotiated with the US Marines at Da Nang airfield to provide an aircraft to fly him south. They readily agreed but their sole condition was that the Aussies organized a pallet of Fosters or Victoria Bitter beer for them, at cost price of course. Sounded like a fair trade.

Of course the flight would also allow the divers to replenish their stocks of Australian beer. The departing team had stressed to the newcomers how important a good stock of Australian beer was for bartering with the Americans. Anything and everything could be obtained through the US system if you had the right item to trade.

Everything went smoothly for Stan until the DC3 took off from Vung Tau on its return journey to Da Nang. The aircraft was heavily loaded with beer and other items the Marines had borrowed, begged and stolen from around the Vung Tau airfield.

For the return trip, a US Marine Padre had bummed a ride with them back to Da Nang. Stan and the Padre were sitting directly behind the flight deck and they both could clearly see what was going on in the cockpit. As Stan told the team on his return,

"We were barreling down the runway and it was obvious that we were a bit overloaded – probably too much beer. As the tail lifted off the ground, I could see the end of the runway and it was getting bloody close. The co-pilot was saying quite loudly, 'C'mon ole girl, c'mon, faster, faster baby.' The padre and I could hear this. So he starts madly crossing himself, saying his Hail Mary's. With barely any runway remaining, the old girl struggled into the air. I looked across at the Padre with a shit grin on my face, pointed upwards, crossed myself and said, 'It worked. He's looking after us'. The silly old bastard couldn't see the funny side at all. No sense of humour these 'God Wallopers'."

Just because they were airborne out of Vung Tau didn't mean their adventure was over. Back in Da Nang, the young ABs were all lounging around watching the Armed Forces network TV news when the phone in John's office rang. After a few minutes John came out and said in a serious tone,

"Stan's plane has crashed - but he's OK."

There was a brief stunned silence before John continued,

"They had an engine failure and diverted to Cam Ranh Bay. Then the gear wouldn't go down so they made a belly landing. The aircraft pranged but no serious injuries, and Stan is fine."

Pete couldn't help himself, *"Thank Christ he's OK, but what about the beer Boss?"*

John shook his head and grinned, *"Yeah, Stan said the beer survived as well."*

They all heaved a collective sigh of relief for both Stan and the beer.

When Willy picked Stan up from the airport next afternoon after he had arrived on a C-130 shuttle service from Cam Ranh Bay, Stan had a grin from ear to ear.

"This place gets more exciting every day."

Willy said, *"We didn't give a shit about you Stan but we were pretty worried about the beer."*

"You're a pack of bastards" he grinned, obviously glad to be back safely amongst his own.

On the drive back to the hooch he mused,

"Think I'll stay in bed or get on the piss for about a week until things calm down a bit. Getting a bit too hectic around here for me."

"Got bad news for you Mate," Willy said, *"we're packing our diving gear now. A chopper flying south this morning from Cua Viet spotted a capsized LCU (Landing Craft Utility) in the surf about 70 klicks north of us. Been missing for a few days. Doesn't appear to be any survivors. She was loaded with ammunition and we're heading up there early tomorrow morning to take a look."*

"Murphy's law Willy. It never rains; it fuckin pours."

replied Stan.

While the big CH-47 Chinook flew two circuits around the landing craft, Willy could see the upturned hull laying parallel to the beach and sitting right in the surf line. Big breakers were pounding her relentlessly, white spray exploding into the air.

Three Armoured Personnel Carriers were harbored up (*parked in a circular defensive perimeter*) in the tree line and from the look of their ponchos strung out between the trees, they had been there for the night.

Amongst a swirl of flying sand the big twin rotor chopper touched down on the beach.

The surf looked a lot more menacing at beach level. The seas were still raging from the last big storm which had also been responsible for running the ammunition barge aground earlier in Da Nang harbour.

As the divers unloaded their gear from the chopper, the biggest tank Willy had ever seen came rumbling up the beach towards them. It was a 'tank retriever'. Big enough and powerful enough to haul other tanks out of any sort of bog. It growled to a halt 50 metres from the Chinook and waited.

The APC crews came down to give the Australians a hand to haul the diving gear up to their camp as the big chopper lifted from the beach, sandblasting everything within a 50 metre radius.

Their senior man was a young Army 2nd Lieutenant and all he had been told was to secure the beach adjacent to the wreck and wait for a

Navy EOD team to arrive. The tank retriever crew had similar orders – be available onsite to assist the EOD team.

"Righto fellas," said John, *"let's take a closer look."*

The LCU had turned turtle and was completely upside down. The scouring action of the surf was already causing the hull to gradually settle deeper in the sand. The waves were breaking across the hull making it very tricky to conduct any sort of immediate inspection.

John weighed up the risks and gains and decided that it was too rough to attempt anything until the surf had subsided a little.

The tank retriever circled up with the APCs and the divers set up their hoochies (*shelters*) within the perimeter. Defensive arrangements for the night were discussed with the APC and tank crews as they were in Charlie country and everyone had to keep their wits about them.

Next morning, with the surf abating, John called an 'O' group to plan their next step. Stan and Willy were to swim out to the stern of the vessel and attach ropes to the propeller 'A' brackets so they at least had a safety line secured from the beach to the hull.

As the surf continued to ease, they were able to take a closer look at the vessel. What they saw didn't give them much encouragement. The wheelhouse structure was completely gone and there was no way the divers could access any part of the hull. All hatches and doors were buried in the sand.

It was obvious that there were no survivors and in all likelihood the entire cargo of ammunition had been lost when she capsized as there was no sign of any cargo in the vicinity of the wreck.

It was assumed she had turned turtle at sea and been driven onto the beach by the heavy seas. John's priority was to recover any bodies and determine the presence of any ammunition or ordnance in the vicinity of the wreck and whether the vessel was salvageable.

They spent the remainder of the morning checking the area surrounding the wreck but found nothing. In the late afternoon, John decided they had seen all they needed to see so called another 'O group' to discuss their next move.

"Nothing more we can do so think we'll wrap this up. Not much four of us can do here. This is really a job for the Navy salvage divers in Da Nang so I think it's time we got out of here. What's the best way to get home LT?"

The young Army 2nd Lieutenant said,

"Our only option is to head straight up the beach back to our base. Charlie would know we are here by now and he knows we have to extract along the beach so we better keep our eyes open. Everybody lock and load. We'll move out with my APC leading, the tank retriever behind me and the other two APCs taking up the rear. Would suggest that your guys load up on the rear vehicle Sir. Everybody stay sharp."

"OK" said John, *"Let's get the fuck out of here."*

As the four vehicles started to roll up the beach, Stan said, *"Wouldn't want to be inside this bloody thing if the shit hits the fan. Everything's out of your control. Like being in a goddamn coffin."*

John replied,

"Yeah true, we had better be ready for anything. We're good target practice sitting up here."

The hatches of all APCs were open with one of the crew manning the .50 caliber machinegun mounted atop the vehicles.

The scrub in the back of beach area was rather stunted but relatively thick. It occurred to Willy that with the setting sun in their faces, the conditions were perfect for Charlie to set an ambush.

They hadn't been underway for more than ten minutes when they heard the roar of an anti-tank round followed by automatic rifle fire up ahead. Miraculously the RPG (*rocket propelled grenade*) had missed the lead APC but a stream of tracer was ripping into them. One of the crew rolled from the top of the vehicle and fell lifeless onto the sand. The .50 caliber machine guns on all APCs immediately opened up.

The Divers' vehicle lurched slightly left and with the engine revs increasing to a roar, accelerated towards the back of beach. The driver had spotted where the fire was coming from and it was pretty obvious that he intended to drive straight over the ambush site.

The lead APC had begun a left hand 140 degree turn and was also heading up the beach towards the source of the tracer as it continued to return suppressing fire with its big .50 cal.

Everyone on board the rear APC opened up on full auto with their M16s hoping to help keep Charlie's head down.

There was no choice, the sailors were going wherever their driver decided to take them. The tank retriever crew apparently had the same intention as they turned left up the beach toward the ambush site. Flames shot from the tank's exhausts like afterburners as the driver opened his throttle wide.

It didn't take long for the VC to realize that if they didn't *'di di mau'* (leave very quickly), they were going to be run over by four steel monsters. They ceased firing and Willy could see a few black pajama clad individuals up and running. That's when it became target practice for the crews.

Within seconds of it beginning, the vehicles were roaring into the scrub as the drivers tried to run down the escaping VC. Everyone aboard the APCs were pouring a huge volume of small arms fire at them and at least six VC went down. Then they were into the ambush site and rolling straight over bodies. The driver of the Aussies' APC had his sights set on one guy who was running for his life. Stan shot him just before he disappeared under the tracks of their APC.

The four track vehicles continued to circle around the perimeter of the ambush site looking for any more sign of men in black pajamas. It appeared that the cavalry charge had managed to get the lot of them.

The lead APC roared back down the beach to

recover their man while the remaining *'tracks'* parked in defensive positions around the perimeter of the ambush site, engines idling and weapons at the ready.

John turned to Stan,

"Stan come with me. Dusty, Willy, stay on top and cover our asses."

They dismounted and cautiously inspected the ambush site for weapons and ordnance. There were seven bodies, all armed with AK47s and John was a little unsettled to discover four unfired RPG-2 rocket launchers. Only the quick reaction of the drivers and the amount of suppressing fire from the .50 cals had saved their butts.

As the search of the bodies for documents continued, the lead APC came gunning up off the beach and pulled up next to John. A young sergeant jumped down and walked over to John,

"Afraid my LT bought it Sir. Rest of my crew are fine."

"Shit!" said John *"OK, let's round up the weapons and any documents you can find and we'll get the hell out of here."*

It was well after dark when the vehicles rolled into the security of the Cavalry compound. Not much had been said during the trip back. Not just because the sailors knew they couldn't relax until they were safely tucked up in the Army compound, but also because all the Aussie divers had taken an immediate liking to the young LT.

The night was spent in the Cav compound and John filled out an after-action report and debriefed the CO while the rest of the Team managed to scrounge a few beers and a meal.

Next morning the CO arranged a chopper for them to get back to Da Nang.

There was a misty fog over the countryside as the chopper lifted off but the pilot just picked up Highway One and flying just above the treetops, followed it all the way back to Da Nang.

As the chopper approached the Hai Van Pass, the fog cleared and they had a spectacular view of the city of Da Nang and its impressive harbour as they flew down off the top of the Pass.

'Tank Retriever' at Tan My.

The overturned LCU at Tan My.

CHAPTER 8

Life settled down for a couple of days after their return. Not knowing what to expect next, the lads took advantage of the much appreciated lull to get to know their American hosts and conduct a bit of a recce around Da Nang.

They soon discovered that the Americans went to war with all the comforts of home. There was a monthly duty free allowances for cigarettes and alcohol, and they could purchase anything they wanted, from Japanese dolls to the latest SLR cameras at duty free prices through the US Post Exchanges in Japan. Their orders were then delivered to them courtesy of the US Military mail system.

The American troops could even order the latest Ford Mustang or Chevy Corvette sports cars tax free to be waiting for them when they arrived Stateside after their 12-month tour.

Pete had said to Willy, *"Going to war with the Yanks ain't too bad at all."*

Dusty had done a deal with one of the US Navy sailors and exchanged a case of Aussie beer for a set of water skis. Before long, Dusty and Willy were out water ski-ing around Da Nang harbour. The Americans assumed they must have been officers so they were never questioned. The Chief turned a blind eye as it gave the diving boat a good run and the boys some much needed relief.

Before their mates in the previous team had departed for Australia, they had recommended that the new Team should always carry a few rounds of dummy explosive ordnance in their vehicles when driving around the city.

The US Military Police came down hard on any troops found on the streets of Da Nang after dark, as they strictly enforced the curfew. The Aussies had written authority to be out at anytime providing they were on an EOD task. The old team's advice paid dividends sooner than was expected. They all realized that EOD was *'double dutch'* to the average US soldier and Australian troops were in a similar category to aliens from another planet. So they soon discovered they had one hell of an advantage over the pedantic US Military Police who regularly patrolled the Da Nang city limits looking for curfew breakers.

The off duty team decided to test the waters one night when they thought it was time to introduce themselves to Da Nang's *'ladies of the night'*. These areas were totally off limits to US personnel and the Military police kept a good lookout for troops who might be tempted to visit these women of ill repute. With the exception of the Boss and Stan, the team headed for *'Red Beach'*, a notorious local area which housed ladies from *'the oldest profession in the world'*.

Being Australian Navy Divers, they quickly found a suitable abode dedicated to putting a smile on the faces of most men. Female company being their chief objective, they settled down to a beer and a bullshit with Mama San and her girls. On this occasion they were wearing Australian greens and Australian rank badges.

They had just begun to settle in and enjoy the company of these lovely ladies when several Military police barged their way through the front door armed to the teeth.

The Chief reacted like greased lightning. He jumped to his feet, and facing the young Military Police Lieutenant with absolute confidence and authority said,

"Who the fuck are you? Don't you know we have an extremely dangerous EOD clearance operation going on here? Get your men the fuck out of here NOW. This area is alive with booby traps. Clear the area ASAP LT."

The utterly confused young Army officer, neither recognizing the rank badges, uniforms or accent took the path of least resistance drummed into him as an officer – if you have no idea what is going on, salute and follow orders.

He snapped to attention, saluted and screamed at his men, *"You heard the officer, move it."*

The Chief had come on so unexpectedly and forcefully to this young LT that he hadn't had time to notice the beer cans on the tables. The ingrained fear of rank and authority had won the day - for the moment.

After the MPs had left, the Chief deciding discretion being the better part of valour said to his boys,

"Let's get the fuck out of here before that kid realizes he's been spun a crock of shit."

Telling the ladies they would return at a more convenient time, they piled into the Jeep and headed back to their hooch on the opposite side of the harbour.

Thankfully, there was a lull in activity over the next several days, giving them time to explore the Da Nang area properly and get their bearings, visit a few of the US bases and make contact with the various US EOD teams in the area. Most importantly, as far as the junior sailors were concerned, they discovered where the best US military clubs and bars were located. Being divers, they quickly made friends with the people who really mattered – bar managers, stores types etc.

They also discovered there were a number of US Red Cross girls (*affectionately referred to as Donut Dollies because they sometimes handed out Donuts to wounded men in the hospitals*) based in the Da Nang area. Dusty and Pete took it upon themselves to follow up this lead and make sure these girls knew there were Aussies in town and that they would be delighted to make their acquaintance at the first opportunity.

Two days later Pete informed the Chief and Stan that six very pretty Donut Dollies were to be their quests the following Saturday for an Aussie style barbecue at the hooch.

Stan asked,

"And who's doing all the preparation and cooking for this little get together?"

Dusty responded,

"Good on ya Stan, you're the best chef in town and we know how you love cooking."

"You pair of bastards, you've set me up. I get the prettiest one, all right?" grinned Stan.

As luck would have it, a request for assistance came in on that Friday afternoon from an Air Cavalry unit based about 100 klicks (*kilometers*) north of Da Nang. They had lost a chopper that morning while it was returning from a fire support mission. It had crashed into a shallow river and there were no apparent survivors. They wanted the Divers to recover the bodies and ordnance before Charlie could get to it.

The Boss decided two could handle the job so he asked for volunteers, knowing the big BBQ and the girls were all set for the following day. It did not take an Einstein to figure out that the Chief and Willy had drawn the short straw. Stan was chief cook for the day and Dusty and Pete had organized the girls so that left just Willy and the Chief.

A chopper from the Air Cav picked the pair up two hours later and they landed at the Air Cav base camp just on dusk.

The CO advised them they would be inserting into the area at first light and proceeded to brief them on what they knew about enemy activity and the wreck site conditions. US Army Rangers would accompany them to provide a protective perimeter, as it was known to be in Charlie territory.

Over a few beers in their mess, Willy and the Chief managed to learn a bit about the Air Cavalry.

This particular unit had eighteen choppers – six UH1 Huey transports (*Slicks*), six Light Observation Helicopters (*LOACHs*) and six Huey Cobra gunships (*Snakes*). Apart from the Commanding Officer and XO, the pilots all appeared to be kids not long out of high school. In fact, most of them were under 21 years of age.

The Aussie divers were soon to learn that first impressions can be very deceiving. These young lads were extremely competent professionals and superb pilots.

The following morning as the first rays of sunlight were streaking the dark green horizon with brilliant flashes of yellow and orange, they were aboard a Huey circling above the downed chopper getting a feel for the lay of the land and the river. The other choppers could be seen skidding into two LZs on either side of the river and disgorging the Ranger security force. All that could be seen of the wreck was a single rotor blade protruding about a foot out of the muddy water.

Once the Ranger unit was in position, the divers' chopper was advised it was clear to land. As the aircraft touched down on the grassy embankment, the Chief and Willy jumped out with their two sets of diving gear and headed for the water's edge. The Ranger Captain followed with his radio operator and set up his HQ in some light cover near the riverbank. With this group was the XO of the Air Cav unit. After setting up their gear on the bank, the Chief said,

"Righto Willy, a quick recce to find out the state of the aircraft and accessibility. Then we'll decide on the

priorities. I'll tend you from here. Be careful. Be very easy to get tangled up as visibility will be zero. When you're ready!"

Willy secured his lifeline and strapped on his dive set, facemask and fins. He waded backwards into the muddy ooze and swam out to the single blade protruding from the water like a beckoning finger. With a last glance at the bank and giving the Chief a thumbs up, Willy left the surface and slowly worked his way down the long flat blade, using his hands to feel his way.

The muddy brown water enveloped him in a dark dirty cloud. He had to actually touch the glass of his facemask just to see his fingers, and then only the dark outline was visible. He could see nothing.

When Willy reached the rotor head it was obvious the chopper was lying at an angle of about 45º. Working his way over the roof of the cabin, he soon found the main side opening but there was no sign of a door. Willy had expected this as choppers in Vietnam rarely had their side doors attached.

Feeling his way forward to begin his search from the front, he came across the first sign of real damage. Part of the fuselage had either been shot away or torn away on impact.

Moving very gingerly Willy came to what he thought was the pilot's compartment. All of the pilot's door appeared to be missing.

Feeling all around with his hands for protrusions that could easily entangle his diving set or lifeline, he carefully entered the cockpit. As he reached through the door, his hand immediately encountered what could only be a flying suit.

Willy's initial reaction was that he wished he were somewhere else. He did not have to move much further before he touched the body of the second pilot. Both were still strapped in their seats.

Moving slowly back to the main cabin Willy began a search for the remaining two crewmen. Inching forward by feel alone and trying to retain the layout of the chopper in his head, he carefully and slowly felt his way around.

The aircraft appeared to be twisted and it was a little difficult to maintain any sense of where he was. Willy found the body of the first crewman relatively easily but the compartment was already coated with slimy mud.

He spent about five minutes to no avail searching for the other crewman. It was long enough. Time to get out of there and let the Chief know what the score was. As he reached the rotor-head assembly, he tugged on his lifeline four times to let the Chief know he was heading for the surface. When Willy broke surface and gave a thumbs up, the Chief pulled him ashore.

The number one priority of the Americans was to recover the bodies of their mates. The chopper and ordnance came second.

When Willy said he had located three of the crew and could get them out, the XO looked very relieved. He had been on the radio to his CO who had advised that a Sky Crane (*Sikorsky CH-54 with a capacity to lift 9 tons*) was available to attempt a recovery of the Huey if the Divers thought it was feasible, but only after the bodies had been recovered. Willy told him recovery was possible as the rotor head appeared to be intact and he would go back in to retrieve the bodies as soon as they were all ready. The XO immediately radioed for two choppers to do a low-level sweep down steam to look for the missing crew member.

The Chief and Willy quickly put together a plan to extract the bodies. Willy would take three lines with him and secure them to the rotor head. Then taking one line at a time he would enter the aircraft, secure it to one of the bodies using a bowline, unbuckle the safety harness and after maneuvering the body clear of the cabin, signal to shore to pull it in. He would need to repeat this three times.

When the last crewman was free, Willy returned to the rotor head to inspect its general condition. Deciding it was worth a try to hoist the chopper, he surfaced and swam ashore.

A Huey was on the ground nearby and he could see the last of the body bags being loaded aboard.

The XO thanked Willy for getting his men out and told him that a chopper had already found and recovered the missing crewman floating about a klick downstream.

He told them,

"We have a CH-54 inbound with lifting strops. Do you still think we can haul it out?"

"The rotor assembly appears to be undamaged and the fuselage is not too deep in the mud, so I think it's worth

a try." replied Willy.

"OK guys, the Sky Crane is going to land first and the pilot will want to discuss with you how he wants the lifting strops attached. He should be here inside 10."

"No worries Sir, I'm ready when you are." Willy said.

They heard the big ugly chopper, which resembled a Preying Mantis insect, before they saw it. It was on descent from about 2,000 feet and off on its starboard quarter like an attentive sheepdog was a Cobra gunship. As the huge heavy lift helicopter came into land, its escort gunship maintained some altitude and began flying a clockwise circuit out beyond the limit of their Ranger perimeter force.

As soon as it had touched down, with the big turbines still whining and blades still turning, the pilot emerged and trotted over to the Aussies, removing his helmet as he came.

Quick handshakes all-round and it was down to business. Willy described the condition of the downed chopper and informed the pilot that it hadn't yet settled too deeply in the muddy quagmire of the river bottom. The pilot in turn went through their lifting procedures and signals.

It was agreed the Chief would be in direct contact via a PRC 25 radio *(VHF FM combat-net radio transceiver)* with the pilot in command throughout the evolution.

When everyone was satisfied with how it was to be done, they walked across to the chopper to inspect the lifting strop and shackles. It was the pilot's intention to attempt a lift to several feet above water level and then gently transfer the wreck across to the bank where he would land again and hook up a more secure lift for transportation back to base.

The pilot gave Willy a thumbs up as he headed back to his heavy lift chopper.

The downdraft from the massive blades and the roar of the turbines directly overhead was unbelievable.

Slowly but steadily, the big chopper maneuvered the heavy strop into position alongside the protruding blade so Willy could attach a line to the lifting gear. He left the surface and sank down to the rotor head.

Once he was in a secure position, he signaled the Chief using his lifeline for the strop to be lowered slowly and the Chief in turn gave directions to the pilot.

Bit by bit the lifting strop came down and using the rope he had attached to the strop, Willy guided it to the rotor head.

Once the shackles were in a position to hook up, Willy took turns around the rotor shaft and signaled; enough. The guy flying that chopper must have been a hell of a pilot because the strop was barely moving.

Just as well, Willy thought. He would be in serious trouble if the steel wire was moving excessively around the wreck in zero visibility and he was in its way. In a few minutes it was all set.

To ensure there would be no snags, Willy signaled to the Chief for the strop to be raised gently.

Slowly and steadily, tension came on the lifting gear. Once the weight had been taken, he signaled - hold. Then, following the strop back to the surface, Willy indicated with a raised thumb that all was OK and began kicking for shore.

Once he was clear of the water, the Chief confirmed to the Sky Crane pilot, *"All clear, it's all yours."* Slowly the pitch of the blades increased, taking more and more of the weight of the downed Huey. The down blast of air generated by the big chopper's blades and resulting spray being blown sideways off the water was staggering.

Ever so slowly the big chopper inched skywards, with more and more of the Huey's blade emerging from the water. The top of the fuselage broke surface and water was cascading from the hull. And then it was clear.

With the precision of a surgeon, the pilot inched the under slung Huey across to the bank and lowered it gently onto the grass.

While the Chief stayed on the radio, Willy moved across to unhook the shackles. From that point it was in the hands of the Sky Crane crew. They landed alongside the Huey, re-rigged the lifting points, hooked up again and were on their way, with the Cobra tucking in behind them for the slow trip back to their base.

That was it. So time for the rest of them to get out of there. A chopper ride back to the Air Cav unit for a shower and a hot brew, and then the flight home.

When Willy and the Chief were ready to leave for Da Nang, the Air Cav CO could not thank them enough. He said,

"I've got a chopper turning up on the pad for you guys. We'll have you back in Da Nang before they even get that BBQ lit. Hope you can impress those Donut Dollies with a couple of good war stories. Some guys have all the luck. If you ever have some time to spare up this way, drop by and I'll get you a joy ride in a Snake if you're interested."

Willy shot back,

"I'll take you up on that offer Sir."

As the Chief and Willy walked into the hooch back in Da Nang, Pete grinned and said,

"Damn, the competition's back in town."

Everyone had obviously had a few drinks as there were grins all round, including the *'Donut Dollies'*. There were six very pretty young American girls and it struck Willy that they looked delighted to see the party now evenly balanced. Pete said he had already told the girls that the two of them would probably not make it back until the following day.

Dusty whispered in Willy's ear with his usual shit grin,

"What did you pair of bastards have to come back for? I reckon I had two of them in the palm of my hand."

Willy laughed,

"Dusty, you wouldn't know what to do with them, apart from buy them drinks all night."

"Fuck off." Dusty chortled as he slapped him on the back, obviously glad to see his mate home safe and

sound.

After introductions all round, John said he and Dusty were taking the duty so the Chief and Willy could get stuck into a drink or two. They didn't need to be told twice. Cold Australian beer, spare ribs barbequed to perfection by Stan and the company of silver tongued Navy divers - the girls loved it.

CHAPTER 9

About a week later they received an invitation from the US Marine EOD team, which was based at the Da Nang airfield, to attend a *'welcome aboard'* party in their honour. It became apparent there were no secrets in the EOD community as the Marines informed the Aussies they were quite welcome to bring along their new found lady friends.

The girls accepted the invitation without hesitation. Dusty and Willy had made quite a hit with two of the girls, Sandra and Rebecca, so all four of them crammed into a Dodge pickup truck with just a single bench seat for what turned out to be a very cozy trip to the Marine EOD hooch.

As the Divers entered the bar with these lovely young ladies on their arms, all conversation died away. It was indeed a rare thing for the average serviceman in Vietnam to even see a *'round eye'*, let alone talk to one up close. They were the hit of the party.

Their EOD allies made them very welcome and the party soon started to warm up. Groups of Marines quickly formed around the girls as every bloke in the bar thought he was in with a chance to win the heart of one of these cute and charming girls. The six Dollies were the only females at the party. No wonder the Marines had wanted the Aussies to bring them.

Being Aussie sailors, they soon got stuck into the free beer and went about making friends with everyone. Being Aussie sailors, they also did what was the custom at home; they drank beer and probably paid less attention to the girls than the girls expected or were accustomed to. It worked like a charm. The less interest the Aussies showed, the more the girls stuck to their sides.

As the night wore on, it didn't take a blind man to see that the Marines didn't stand a chance. The sailors from 'Down Under' were young, extremely fit and had Aussie accents, and they probably behaved unlike any males the girls had ever met.

John and the senior Marine Chief Warrant Officer hit it off as if they had been mates for years. Both were smoking huge cigars and drinking copious quantities of Chivas Regal Scotch whisky.

When it came time to head back to their hooch, Dusty, Willy and their two lady friends jumped into the pickup truck for the trip home. It had been a great night and both of them were 'seven sheets to the wind' (under the weather). Willy was at the wheel and as they drove along the concrete culvert lined road which circumnavigated the airport, Rebecca decided she would give his ear a bit of a nibble. Being easily distracted by the female sex, Willy turned his head towards her. Their kiss lingered a little longer than either of them expected, so Willy was completely distracted from the fact that he was in charge of a vehicle doing about 35 mph, at night, while under the influence of the demon drink.

He thought it must have been her kiss, but the sensation of the vehicle slowing rotating through the air became increasingly more noticeable. Then with a thud and screech of metal, the pickup was at a 50-degree angle and sliding to a rapid halt in the deep concrete culvert. Willy was pressed against the driver's door with two lovely females lying on top of him, and Dusty somewhere above them all. Dusty broke into his usual shit grin as Willy said,

"What the fuck, over?"

Dusty laughed and said,

"You dickhead, we're in the goddamn drain."

Willy asked the girls if they were OK, and after they both started to giggle nervously, he said to Dusty,

"I don't believe this shit. Wind down your window mate so we can get the hell out of here."

With the vehicle on its side, it was a bit of a scramble before they all managed to climb out. Being on the bottom, Willy had several footprints on his face by the time they were all clear. As he climbed out the window, the first face he saw was that of the Chief, and he was glaring directly at Willy.

He, along with Stan and two of the girls, had been following along behind in one of the Team's Jeeps and had watched in amazement as the pickup had leisurely veered off the road and into the concrete culvert. The Chief said, in a less than happy voice,

"You pair of wankers! What the hell happened?"

"Buggered if I know Chief. Think there might have been a bit of a problem with the steering." Willy replied.

"Jesus. The Boss is going to be pissed off. This is a brand new vehicle. Useless pair of bastards."

After Stan got on the radio and reported the damaged vehicle, all eight of them wedged themselves into the Jeep and headed for home. With his usual grin, Stan chuckled,

"Can't leave you pair of wankers alone for five minutes without you getting in the shit."

It turned out that John was not impressed. Dusty and Willy spent the following week on full-time duty and stoppage of all alcohol. Such is life they say.

After this exciting little escapade at the airfield, their workload began to pick up again.

The night following the vehicle incident, they received a call from Harbour Security at about 0300 informing them that enemy sapper swimmers had been sighted at the Deep Water ammunition piers. A sentry had caught sight of two Vietnamese nationals on the upper deck of a US Ammunition ship and when spotted, they had jumped over the side to be picked up by a waiting motorized sampan which then disappeared into the night at a great rate of knots.

Fifteen minutes later, Stan, Dusty and Willy arrived at the piers with red light flashing and siren blaring. The senior NCO of the security police detachment quickly briefed the divers on the little information he had gathered.

The bad news was that the ship in question carried over 10,000 tons of high explosive ordnance and it was unknown how long the two Viets may have been onboard before they were sighted. They had a minimum of 25 minutes head start on the Team so the divers had to assume the intruders had successfully placed a sabotage device somewhere aboard the vessel.

There wasn't any good news. Upper deck sentries had fired shots at the intruders but they had apparently escaped unharmed.

Prior to the arrival of the EOD team, security had taken the precaution of clearing the vessel and wharf area of all personnel. Assuming any delayed sabotage device would function somewhere between 30 minutes to one hour after being armed, they did not have a lot of time to procrastinate.

Stan confirmed the exact location where the intruders were last seen and instructed the Security NCO to get his men as far as possible away from the ship. He turned to the rest of his lads and said,

"The bad news fellas, is we don't have any choice but to go onboard and check the area where these sappers were last seen. I don't have to tell you that if they have planted anything, we need to find it pretty damn quick. Let's go."

EOD tools kits in hand, they climbed the vessel's gangway with Stan leading the way. Willy had to admit to himself, he felt a little like a condemned man taking his final walk to the gallows.

Only an EOD operator can fully comprehend the indescribably eerie and lonely feeling associated with searching a ship loaded to the gunwales with thousands of tons of high explosives, in the middle of the night, knowing that a fanatical enemy saboteur has recently been aboard.

Of course they had no choice but to attempt to find the device and neutralize it. There was too much at stake. Were it to detonate, not only would the ship and its cargo be lost, but also the ammunition piers would be utterly destroyed and two other ammunition vessels alongside the wharf would most probably be lost as well.

This was what the Aussie CDs were paid $14 per fortnight danger money for!!!

Willy's momentary qualms quickly faded as he refocused on the job in hand. The odds may have been a long way from ideal but he was with two of his mates whom he trusted unconditionally, not only for their professionalism, but also for their cool heads when under pressure. They all had a pretty good idea of Charlie's methods so knew what to look for.

Fortunately when the crew had evacuated the vessel, they had left all upper deck lighting switched on.

The CDs headed directly for the area where the sappers had last been sighted. They soon picked up a trail of small puddles of water on the deck leading from the ship's side to the nearest stack of pallets on the upper deck. Secured to the lower rung of the guardrail and hanging over the side was a length of rope reaching all the way to the waterline.

Following the water trail, they cautiously moved amongst the stacked pallets, all loaded with 500-pound bombs. Stan was focusing on retracing the sapper's footsteps while Dusty and Willy scanned to either side, making sure they missed nothing.

Apart from their footsteps on the steel deck, the only sound was the steady hum of the ship's ventilators. In a firm but steady voice Stan abruptly declared,

"Got it."

Dusty and Willy froze in their tracks. Stan was pointing at an olive drab coloured canvas bag wedged in between the noses of two 500 pounders. The little bastards had even used a US manufactured canvas bag normally used for carrying plastic explosives. He turned to his two mates and said,

"Dusty, you keep checking all the surrounding pallets. Willy, you stay with me."

As Dusty moved off, Stan was thinking aloud,

"Chances of it being booby trapped are pretty low. I reckon they would have been in a hell of a hurry, but sure as eggs, there will be a time delay of some sort and time will be getting short."

Stan opened his EOD kit and Willy nodded his agreement,

"Agreed. We better get a move on before the bastard cooks off."

While Willy held the large powerful torch, Stan began gently cutting open the side of the bag with a Stanley knife, being extremely careful not to disturb the bag or its contents. As the hole gradually widened, Stan stated what was clearly obvious to them both,

"Det cord wrapped around C-4. Gotta be some sort of time pencil and blasting cap in here as well."

Detonating cord is a plastic coated cord containing the high explosive PETN. C-4 is a plasticized high explosive consisting of mainly RDX explosive. The Det cord was to be the means of detonating the C-4 which in turn would detonate the pallet of bombs.

Somewhere in the bag they knew would be the time delay device attached to a blasting cap which would initiate the cord, thus setting of the detonation sequence.

Because it was in intimate contact with one of the bombs, the C-4 was sufficiently powerful to detonate it which in turn would detonate the pallet of 500 pound bombs. These in turn would set off the neighbouring pallets which would be sufficient to probably *'cook off'* the entire ship's cargo of high explosive ordnance. This entire sequence would take place within the space of a few microseconds. Moreover, if the Team were unable to prevent it from happening, they would know nothing about it as they would all be instantly vaporized.

Gently slicing open more of the bag, Stan declared,

"No sweat. Just as we thought. A time pencil and

blasting cap, Det cord with half a dozen turns around the C-4. Just a matter of cutting the cap and pencil away. You happy with that Willy?"

"Looks good to me. Let do it."

Willy handed Stan a crimping tool, which being non-ferrous, was safe to cut detonating cord. One firm snip and it was done. Stan handed Willy the time pencil with the blasting cap with several inches of Det cord still attached. Gingerly, Willy headed straight for the ship's side and heaved it into the night. When he got back to Stan's location, he nodded *"Done"*.

Dusty was just giving the all clear as Stan carefully extracted the entire canvas bag and its contents. A quick examination revealed nothing more than approximately a 20 pound bundle of C-4 with the bulk of the det cord still wrapped around it. Completely safe now that the blasting cap had been removed.

Stan turned and grinned at the others,

"Thank Christ that's done. A cold beer would go down well."

"Sure would beat the shit out of standing around here." replied Dusty.

As they approached the gangway of the ship, they all heard and felt a short dull thud. Clearly the time pencil had just functioned on the seabed, 40 feet below the ship, firing the blasting cap and the cord. They all stopped as one and looked at each other. It was clear to all that they had been within a few minutes of meeting their maker.

Stan grinned and said,

"Close one!!"

Stan advised the Security NCO of what they had found and that their professional opinion was the intruder had only placed the single charge. Stan's parting comment to the senior Security Petty Officer was very clear and to the point -

"Mate, I suggest you light a very big fucking fire under your sentries. You came within a hair's breadth of seeing 10,000 tons of high explosive go sky high. That would have been enough to upset everyone's day - especially ours."

The sensation of reprieve as they drove out the wharf gates is not easy to describe, suffice to say they all felt utterly exhausted. Once again they had beaten the odds. No one said a word.

John was waiting for them when they arrived back at the hooch. They sat down to a cold beer as Stan filled the Boss in with the details.

The three of them were in agreement that a Vietnamese national working aboard the vessel must have secured the line hanging over the side, allowing the two sappers to climb onboard with their explosive charge. They must have swum in, hence the water trail on the deck. John agreed it was the only logical conclusion and went to his office to prepare his report for the OIC of Harbour Security.

There was obviously a VC sympathizer working at the ammunition piers.

When Willy reached for his beer, he noticed for the first time that his hands were trembling. The adrenaline had worn off, and the reality of just how close a thing it was, had begun to dawn on him.

After a close call with the *'Grim Reaper'*, the human mind takes time to confront and deal with the full extent of the danger just faced. This was not their first near miss but they seemed to be coming at them just a little too thick and fast.

The funny thing was, none of them ever talked about what was going through their own minds during and after these ongoing series of narrow escapes.

The night's events were already history and there was no time to dwell on it. They knew they had to be mentally prepared for the next call, not dwell on the last one.

CHAPTER 10

Life for the Team was not *'all work and no play'*. They had their quiet days when they could kick back and relax, have a few beers and socialize with their American mates and the Donut Dollies.

They quickly established a very close relationship with the US Navy Underwater Demolition Teams (*UDT*), SEAL teams and of course US EOD teams.

The US EOD sailors had a saying which the Aussie Divers felt succinctly covered their own mind-set. *'Can Do Easy'* was soon adopted as their unofficial motto. It summed up their conviction that no job was too tough or beyond their ability.

Another of Willy's favorites was one used by US Navy SEALS - *'The only Easy Day was Yesterday'*. To him it meant a couple of things; yesterday was done, today is another day and chances are, it may be worse, and never take for granted that things will get easier. Be prepared for the worst outcome – a very healthy outlook in his opinion.

The US Navy SEALS also had a particularly positive attitude amongst themselves. It was summed up by their motto:

"Yea, though I walk through the Valley
of the Shadow of Death,

I fear no evil, for I am the meanest
mutha-fucker in the Valley."

The Aussies made their hooch a haven from the war and always kept an open door to all branches of the Special Warfare community, whether they wanted to drop in for a meal, grab a bunk for the night, or just to *'shoot the shit'* over a few cold Aussie beers.

On the odd occasion they had visitors who quickly wore out their welcome. One such incident occurred when the Divers had a party for a group of Australian entertainers who were visiting Da Nang with a USO (*United Services Organization*) tour. Groups of singers, dancers and band members who toured the US bases throughout South Vietnam to entertain the troops.

Several administrative type US Navy officers – REMFs - from the base had heard about their little party and had decided to show up uninvited. Initially no-one was too concerned. A few extras here and there didn't matter much. They had plenty of beer and tucker.

As the evening wore on however, one of the more junior officers, a Lieutenant JG (junior grade), who incidentally was trying to win the heart of an Australian dancer, started behaving as if he were in his officer's mess. Willy had the duty, so was stone cold sober.

All was going well until this stroppy little officer tapped Willy on the shoulder and told him to get himself and the young lady another drink. Willy casually told him to *"Piss off and get your own fucking drink."* and turned back to resume his conversation with Pete.

As Willy was wearing no rank badges, the officer assumed (quite rightly) that he was only a sailor and felt that he should jump to it at his command. To make matters worse, when Willy had effectively told him to go *'take a jump'* in front of the young attractive female, his ego was trampled.

His next line of attack was to put the big Aussie in his place by reminding him that he was talking to a Naval officer. That was about as much as Willy intended to put up with so he responded with,

"Tell the Chaplain Sir - he might give a fuck, because I don't."

Well, you would have thought someone had stuck a broom up his ass. He flushed a brilliant red and started to stutter that he would have the Aussie charged with insubordination. Willy felt the time had come. He took him firmly by the upper arm and pointed him towards the door. The shocked officer didn't resist as he was completely stunned by the unexpected response.

When they were outside the bar, Willy looked down at him and said in a firm tone,

"First point sir - you are a guest here, and an uninvited one at that. Second point – I suggest you learn some manners. Third point – fuck off before I get really pissed off."

The Lt JG looked at this insubordinate sailor for a moment with his mouth hanging open, did an *'about face'* and departed as gracefully as he could manage under the circumstances.

When Willy re-entered the bar, Pete came over to him with a face-splitting grin,

"Jesus Mate, you were a bit tough on that poor little bastard."

Willy broke into a grin and replied,

"Gotta teach them while they are young Mate. He'll think twice now before he tries to big note himself in front of a sheila at the expense of a sailor."

Pete laughed,

"Yeah, but we're in deep shit if he's the victualing officer."

"If I ever run into him again, I bet he'll apologize to me."

Willy felt a big hand on his shoulder and turned to see Stan grinning.

"I saw that. You pair of pricks up to your old tricks eh? You two will get us kicked out of this fuckin' war zone."

"Just doing our bit to educate the junior officers Stan." Willy replied with a wide grin.

As Stan turned away, he countered with a shit eating smirk, *"Yeah, well do it on someone else's watch. You bastards are going to give me goddamn ulcers, or get me hung."*

A few night later, the Chief, Stan, Dave and Willy, ignoring the US curfew, were leaving a hotel bar downtown and as they walked towards their Jeep in the parking compound, they spotted several *'White Mice'* hassling a young girl. She was very distraught and very frightened.

Being Aussies, as one they decided to go to the aid of the damsel in distress. When the Chief asked the police what was going on, they told the Aussie divers in very threatening and impolite terms that it was police business and they should leave before they were arrested as well.

The team knew that it was common practice for these *'official'* thugs to arrest young girls off the street on some ludicrous charge, take them back to the police station and gang-rape them.

Discretion being the better part of valour, the divers quietly backed off and headed for their vehicle from where they watched one of the policemen force the girl onto the back of his motorcycle and take off, presumably heading for the station. His mates remained, most probably to round up a few more young girls.

With the lights of their vehicle switched off, the divers tucked in about 50 metres behind the motorcycle and followed it until they were well clear of the hotel area.

The Chief was driving and once they had reached a deserted street, he accelerated past the bike cutting it off and forcing it into the gutter. The policeman immediately began screaming obscenities at them and making threats.

Believing he had the upper hand, he reached for his .38 handgun, but before it cleared his holster he was staring down the barrels of four cocked Colt .45s, all of which had *'one up the spout'* and were aimed directly at a spot between the mongrel's eyes.

It was probably at that moment that his bowels let go, as with some justification, it dawned on him that he may have been about to join his illustrious ancestors.

Willy knew that if the little mongrel had moved so much as a hair, four 45s would have barked as one. In actual fact, the Aussies were hoping he would move, as they really despised these corrupt and totally evil little bastards.

Stan told the young lady to get into the Jeep and suggested to the police officer that he *'di di mau'* (leave very quickly). Needless to say he took off like a cut snake.

As they were quite close to the US Army's EOD compound they stopped in for a beer and after explaining what had happened, they left the girl in the Army's able care.

The senior NCO's parting comment to them was *'crazy fucking Aussies'*.

They were to later discover that their damsel in distress was in fact a member of the *'oldest profession in the world'*.

After they had departed the Army hooch, she offered her services to all the blokes at Army EOD. They weren't even offered a discount.

When they found out, the Aussies had a bit of a chuckle about it, but they still felt they had done the right thing.

During slack periods the junior sailors of the team regularly roamed the various US military bases seeing what they could beg, borrow or steal. They believed in having lots of *'come in handy'* gear.

On one such occasion, Dusty and Pete felt they could do with a new air conditioner (there were already five installed around the hooch) so Pete and Dusty found out where they should start their search.

It was a large and highly secure compound with wooden boxes and crates stacked high. They introduced themselves to the head *'honcho'* and fed him a line of bullshit about how basic their living conditions were and how desperate they were for some air-con. The NCO pointed to a huge stack of wooden crates in the yard and said,

"You guys just go over there and take your pick."

Life was improving by the day.

Their daily routine ran very close to the edge at times but that was no reason why they should not live in comfort and enjoy their off-time.

Dusty went out of his way to become good friends with the on base Chief Victualer. The Americans brought in cases of frozen prime cut steaks, ice cream, flavored milk, gallon cans of Pacific oysters, gallon cans of dehydrated prawns and so on. Dusty made sure they had copious quantities of nothing but the best.

The Divers had a brick barbeque in their back yard so steaks and prawns were on the evening menu several times a week.

Visiting US EOD and SEAL sailors were amazed at how the Aussies managed to live so well. Most of the food they procured was normally earmarked for the Officers' Messes.

As a result, they acquired a reputation as being the biggest *'shithawks'* in country. If the Aussies couldn't get it, it couldn't be *'got'*.

Life for the Team continued to move along at a

steady pace. There was always someone asking for assistance somewhere in I Corp.

Apart from the salvage operations, which the Divers considered their *'bread and butter'* ops, most calls were at very short notice. In some cases a chopper was already inbound to the nearest chopper pad before they had even received a request for their services.

Such a case was from the Military port authority at Chu Lai, to the south of Da Nang. A large volume of equipment and ordnance came in through this port and like Da Nang, was often a target for VC saboteurs.

On this occasion, a large ordnance carrying Naval vessel lying at anchor awaiting its turn to unload had become a target. Swimmers were spotted and as usual, had gotten clean away.

After a brief chopper ride, three of the Team arrived at the wharf expecting a fast boat to be waiting for them. True to form, no one at the wharf knew anything about it, and to make matters worse, they didn't give damn. A ship sitting at anchor with a possible explosive device attached to her hull did not appear to be very high on their personal list of priorities.

Unfortunately, the Aussies were to witness this very unprofessional attitude a little too often amongst some of the rear echelon US Military. Fortunately, being Aussies with attitude and being EOD, they could usually manage to get their point of view across.

Stan collared the young Lt. JG in charge who

wasn't too excited about lending them one of his boats. Stan in his usual manner let him know what he expected.

"Lieutenant, there is a ship sitting at anchor in your harbour with a shitload of explosives on board and it has been reported to us that it has been attacked by VC swimmers. That means it could go fucking bang anytime. If we don't have our asses out there within the next 5 minutes, I would suggest that your career and your ass will be swinging in the breeze – big time."

They got the boat, but almost two hours had elapsed since the swimmer had been reportedly sighted.

This was an ongoing problem for the Team, as the US Navy had no procedures in place whereby a ship could respond immediately to deal with this type of threat. They carried no divers so they were virtually in the lap of the gods if a charge had been placed on the hull.

The Aussies were the only EOD qualified diving team in I Corp and by the time they arrived on site in these situations, they had to conduct a search during that critical time window when the charge was most likely to function. That was not their preferred option.

The Captain of the vessel was waiting for them and obviously a little concerned - with some justification. After he briefed the team, Stan told him,

"This might be your lucky day Sir. I would suggest that if the charge has not detonated after 2 hours, it has either malfunctioned, or they didn't manage to get anything

onto your hull."

As the swimmer had been spotted near the bows, Stan told the skipper,

"My boys will do a quick search of your anchor cable and then a sweep down both sides of the hull with a final look at the stern area. If you can shut down all seawater pumps and confirm your shafts are locked, we'll get on with it."

Dusty entered the water and immediately disappeared out of sight down the ship's anchor cable. Less than sixty seconds later, he was back on the surface.

"There's a rope at about 15 feet attached to the anchor cable. It is streaming back down the port side. Looks like we've got something."

Stan replied, *"Righto Dusty, do you think you can follow it back without disturbing the line?"*

"Yeah, there's not too much current so no sweat."

"OK, take it easy. We'll lay back off the cable and drift down behind you."

Stan picked up the radio provided by the ship.

"Captain we've found a rope attached to your cable approximately 15 feet below the surface and it's laying back along your port side. We are now following it back along the hull. Can you re-confirm all non-essential personnel are topside. Will keep you advised."

After about 60 feet, Dusty's bubbles stopped moving aft. Whatever it was, he had found it.

They held the boat just forward of his position and waited. Dusty's head appeared at the stern of the boat and he removed his mask and mouthpiece.

"We've got a flotation bladder supporting, my guess, a

50 pound charge under the bilge keel. I can see a simple time fuse that's been fired but appears to be a dud. I've cut the fuse. It's a very basic setup so reckon we can just bring the charge up."

"Righto Dusty, take your time. Attach this line to it, then puncture the bladder and let it drop away from the hull. Then we'll haul it up."

"On my way." said Dusty as he ducked below the surface again, rope in hand.

Within a few minutes Stan and Willy were carefully hauling the charge inboard.

Dusty was right on the money. It was no more than a container of high explosives with an initiator consisting of an igniter, about 20 feet of safety fuse and a detonator. The fuse had burnt down to within a few inches of the detonator but had misfired because of a poor seal between the fuse and detonator which had allowed saltwater to seep into the last few inches of black powder. Damp powder does not burn.

Once again, the VC's quite basic knowledge of demolitions had saved the day.

The Captain was a very relieved man. Stan offered some advice on how he could improve his defensive measures against this type of attack in the future. The Captain was a little taken aback,

"Goddamn it. You people have taught me more in 5 minutes about this shit than my own Navy has taught me in 25 years. I sure do appreciate it."

They left, taking the explosive device with them. After thanking a sheepish boats officer for his help, they chased down the nearest Army EOD

113

team who happily took the now safe explosive charge and locked it away for later disposal. Dusty had removed the blasting cap prior to the charge being hauled onboard the boat.

The Army guys insisted they couldn't leave without partaking of some traditional EOD hospitality. They had already checked on the chopper ride home and said there was an hour or more to spare, so how could the Aussies say no.

And so went another day in *'paradise.'*

Willy could see a major change taking place in his Team mates. The *'newness'* and perhaps initial apprehension that they had all felt in the first few days and weeks in the war zone had long been replaced by a total confidence in their own abilities and in each other. They had all confronted and dealt with a diversity of hazardous situations and in so doing had molded into a very tight and highly professional team.

There was no sign of complacency, just a growing trust in their training, in each other and their ability to do the job.

That aside, they were all enjoying the hell out of it.

When confronted by life threatening situations, there is a huge rush of adrenalin, and it is addictive.

Not until later years were they to look back and fully comprehend that this period was the high point of their young lives.

Never again would they experience such surges of adrenalin, the camaraderie, being at the *'top of the mountain'* - the feeling of being totally alive.

CHAPTER 11

No two days were the same. False alarms became a common part of their daily routine.

Some calls bordered on paranoia and some were very legitimate reactions to an unfamiliar event or circumstance.

Officers who feared their troops may be trying to kill them called the Aussies in to check their hooches, office telephones, or check their vehicles because of their fear of *'Fragging'*.

Fragging did in fact happen when some screwed up sad individual, who for whatever reason, decided that his own hysterical fear, hatred of the Army or dread of being in Vietnam could be resolved by injuring or murdering his superior officer.

It was commonly attempted with a standard issue hand grenade. In many cases, a grenade would be found under a cot or laying in a corner of a locker. Of course no one would touch it – they would call for EOD. Often the response team would find that the officer had himself inadvertently left it lying about and had suffered a memory lapse.

One very bizarre request for assistance came from an Army hospital. Two either extremely bored or extremely stupid soldiers had decided that a *'high'* might be obtained from swallowing C-4 plastic explosives. They were both in a deep coma and the doctors were at a loss as what to do.

So they called EOD. None of the Team had a clue. The effects of eating explosives were way outside of the CDs' line of expertise.

In order to gain more exposure as to how their US allies operated, team members took every opportunity to deploy with other units throughout the length and breadth of South Vietnam.

They spent time with US advisors on the DMZ and worked with Marine, Air force and Army EOD teams all over the war zone.

On one such occasion, Willy deployed to Cam Ranh Bay for a week with the US team stationed there. They lived in a Quonset hut located within 20 metres of the water's edge.

Surrounded by brilliant white sand and crystal clear water, it was a paradise. There was a beach volleyball court set up immediately outside the front door and a large well used BBQ. Willy thought, *'This is going to be all right'*.

During the early afternoon of his first day, after a few games of volleyball, Willy was informed it was time for them to catch their dinner. With a boatload of diving gear, they headed out through the mouth of the harbour and turned south down the rocky coastline.

With perfect visibility Willy was astounded by the number of crayfish feelers he could see waving from the rocky crevices. Before long they had enough crays to feed 30 men.

Back to the hooch as the sun was sinking and out came the salads and rolls while the cray tails were sizzling in butter on the barbeque. Thinking to himself, *'It doesn't get any better than this'*, Willy innocently asked, *"Got any beer Chief?"*

"The day's not over yet Willy. We've still got a bit of work to do."

The Chief suggested that after eating, Willy should get his head down for a couple of hours as he would be taking part in a routine boat patrol after midnight.

Willy was about to discover that although these boys were EOD, their weapons training and boat skills made them the ideal choice of the local Naval Commander to conduct patrols of the harbour during curfew hours to interdict illegal boat traffic.

Anything on the harbour during curfew hours was deemed to be running VC personnel, weapons or supplies.

Willy was awakened at midnight. It was all happening. The black skimmer with the 85hp outboard was being loaded with ammunition boxes, rations, a starlight scope and weapons. It looked like it might be a long night.

After a detailed brief by the senior Chief, they checked their weapons – Willy was given a *'Grease Gun'* (M3 American .45-caliber submachine gun). Also included in the arsenal were two M16s, a pump action shotgun and an M79 40mm grenade launcher.

Four of them, including the boat coxswain, were going out this night. They were to quietly head over to the far shoreline of the harbour, shut down their motor and just drift in the darkness, waiting for some unsuspecting boat unwise enough to break the curfew.

It was a dark night with no moon, just a few stars visible through the scattered overcast.

They were close enough to the shoreline to be invisible to any boat creeping through the darkness. It was the first time Willy had used a starlight scope. Looking through it, everything took on an eerie green haze, but the visibility was amazing. Nothing would get past them this night.

They settled down to wait. Two hours had ticked by and not a word had been spoken. They became part of the night, their senses intensifying as every minute ticked by.

Almost indiscernible at first, the faint *'putt putt'* of a small diesel engine intruded upon the dark stillness and grew louder. It was heading their way. At this late hour it had to be the opposition, and more than likely, they were up to no good.

Ron, the Chief in charge of their little sortie, switched on the night scope and pressed it firmly to his eye. The amount of light generated by the scope was like a beacon in the night so it was imperative that a good seal was obtained against the eye of the user.

He whispered *"5 minutes"* and gave the waiting crew the thumbs up confirming they were in a good position.

The curfew breaker was going to pass them to seaward, making their skimmer virtually invisible against the black shoreline. As the EOD team was working in what was classified as a *'free fire zone'*, they had been instructed to initiate action if they had the upper hand rather than challenge an intruder and lose the element of surprise.

Not knowing what weapons the other boat may be carrying, the team had to gain the upper hand very quickly and maintain it. The only way to do that was to unleash a shitload of firepower over a very short period of time and inflict maximum damage.

They had no option but to assume the approaching boat was hostile.

Steadily the sound of the diesel grew louder. They were confident they would spot the curfew breaker first. Not only did they all have the direction of the intruder pinpointed, it was clear the suspected VC would be silhouetted against the open water and lighter horizon. With luck their white bow wave would also be visible.

Ron whispered, *"one minute"*. The sound of the motor was growing rapidly in intensity. It seemed as if they were going to run down the EOD skimmer.

Then suddenly it was there, slicing across their beam no more than 30 metres away. What appeared to be a regular Vietnamese fishing boat – with no lights visible. All the team had near perfect fields of fire and were waiting for the Chief to initiate the ambush.

Ron yelled *"Go"* and a split second later he opened up on full auto with his M16. The rest of the crew immediately followed suit.

Tracer rounds at night make it relatively easy to direct fire onto a visible target. The M79 thumped twice and it was over as quickly as it had begun. The diesel engine died after the first explosion and there was deathly silence.

The team waited, watching for the slightest movement on the fishing vessel.

Surprisingly, no fires had broken out. On instructions from the Chief, the boat coxswain fired up the outboard and idled towards the lifeless vessel. Assuming nothing, expecting the worst, everyone kept their guard with weapons at the ready as they closed the gap. As Willy had the shorter barreled automatic weapon, Ron motioned for him to board first. Willy thought, *'Good on ya Mate, I'm supposed to be a goddamn guest here'.*

While the American sailors covered his butt, Willy eased himself aboard, eyes scanning everywhere and ears tuned for the slightest sound. The wheelhouse had been completely demolished by a direct hit with a 40mm round. Pretty obvious no one was alive at that end. Turning to the bow, he inched forward, towards the main hold.

The Aussie EOD sailor could make out the shadowy forms of two bodies crumpled on the deck. Behind him he heard one of the other sailors climbing onboard. They were all carrying a couple of small hand grenades which were about the size of golf balls. They had a very small radius of damage but their blast effect was ideal for this situation.

The other sailor, now alongside Willy, whispered, *"I'm going to drop a grenade in the hold."*

Willy replied, *"Roger, moving back."*

The US sailor then pulled the pin and lobbed the grenade through the hatch calling, *"Grenade in the hold, take cover."*

Deftly stepping several paces back the way he had come, Willy flattened himself against the deck, closed his eyes and held his ears. The sharp blast was quite confined in the hold. He felt the thump and waited for the smoke to clear.

Moving forward again, Willy switched on his torch. His night vision was unaffected by the red glow from the torch so he had a clear view of the carnage.

The two bodies on the upper deck were young males and both were dressed in *'black pajamas'*. At their sides were AK47 assault rifles. Willy felt some relief as that confirmed they were VC and not innocent fishermen.

Moving to the hatch, he completed a quick sweep of the hold with the torch. Another two bodies, both female, also in traditional black pajamas. An assortment of items, including food, weapons and ammunition were stacked in the smelly hold.

Ron radioed Harbour Security to send a larger vessel to take the fishing boat in tow back to their base. They would want to thoroughly search the vessel for documents and examine the illicit cargo.

A faint orange glow was spreading across the eastern horizon as the EOD vessel parted company with Harbour Security and their boat coxswain opened the throttles, pushing the skimmer up onto the plane. After several hours of strain and relative discomfort, it was a welcome relief to feel the breeze in their faces again.

Willy was trying hard not to dwell on what had just taken place. Time to come to grips with it later after the Op was over.

As he got his bearings Willy realized they were not heading for the EOD base but towards a beachside village just outside the Naval base. He turned and caught the eye of the Chief, raising his hands to question where they were headed. Ron yelled over the noise of the big outboard, *"Breakfast."* and pointed to the village lying directly over the bow.

In the soft grey light of dawn the boat coxswain nudged the bow of the skimmer onto the pristine white sand. They were obviously expected as a middle aged Mamasan appeared at the doorway of the nearest dwelling with a friendly grin. Ron walked up to her and enveloped her in a huge hug.

As they entered the house, the distinctive aromas of Vietnamese cooking permeated the air. The main room of the house was set up as a little bar with several stools alongside a chest high wooden bench. There was an American brand refrigerator with a large carved wooden EOD badge and a US flag hanging on the wall.

As Willy took in the surroundings, the other lads slumped into soft well worn couches.

Mamasan, still with her cheese eating grin, opened the refrigerator and started passing out ice cold bottles of '33' beer.

Ron turned to Willy and said,

"Welcome Mate to home away from home. This is our place."

Mamasan, looking the Aussie up and down enquired,

"This one new. What his name?"

Grinning, Ron replied,

"He Uc Dai Loi from Da Nang. Name Willy."

"Ahhh", said Mamasan knowingly, *"No problem, have plenty girl. Uc Dai Loi number one."*

Over their first beer, Ron explained that the Navy EOD Team had made this place *'their bar'* and they frequented it on a regular basis, at all hours of the day and night. Breakfast here was part of their nightly routine.

As Willy opened his second beer, four very pretty girls came in carrying plates of cooked seafood, rice and the delicious Vietnamese bread rolls called *'Banh Mi'*. Simmering away in a rich creamy sauce were large prawns and crayfish tails. It looked magnificent and smelt even better.

The young Aussie broke into a smile from ear to ear when a very pretty young lady sat down next to him and began serving him his breakfast.

He couldn't quite believe it. Only an hour or so earlier, they had carried out an ambush where 5 people had been killed. Yet here they were, all drinking beer in a bar on the beach watching a new day dawn, with Willy being hand fed by a gorgeous young Vietnamese lass who was presumably willing to do whatever his heart desired.

It was totally surreal. His emotions were running in all directions. The faces of the dead Viet Cong women were still imprinted on his mind. They would never have another meal; they would never again feel the warmth of another human being; they would never again see their loved ones.

Then he glanced around at the American sailors sitting with him in that house of ill repute. They were grinning and laughing and he thought to himself, *'a great bunch of blokes'*.

After all, those VC were the enemy and they wouldn't be losing any sleep if it had been the EOD team who had been killed and they who had survived the night. Plenty of time later to confront his thoughts and sort out his feelings.

Willy was with some good blokes, enjoying a great feed and sitting next to a gorgeous young lady. It didn't get any better than that.

Over the following week, they repeated this routine on three other occasions, always finishing with breakfast on the beach. Willy was pleased that they never had a repeat of the first night.

He wasn't particularly comfortable with the memory of the two dead young women in the hold.

CHAPTER 12

When Willy arrived back in Da Nang, Dusty was sorting his orders for R&R, or *'Rest and Recreation'* leave.

Their US allies gave all servicemen stationed in Vietnam 7 days leave during their tour. Using chartered civilian airlines (at that time, Pan-Am Boeing 707 jets) troops were given a choice of destinations including Honolulu and Sydney and most of the major cities of SE Asia.

Dusty decided he would take his leave in Hong Kong. Willy was particularly envious of him as he drove Dusty out to catch the C-130 to Saigon, from where he would pick up a direct Pan Am charter flight to *'Honkers'*. With the exception of Pete, they had all visited Hong Kong on Aussie warships and it was a particularly popular destination for all sailors the world over.

"You better come back you bastard. I've had a gutful of carrying your workload while you are here, let alone while you're away on the piss, smooth talking all those little honeys in Lockhart Road." said Willy.

Dusty replied,

"No sweat Mate, I'm going to keep looking until I find that old girlfriend of yours in the Suzie Wong bar and then I'm going to shack up with her for a week. Then I'm

going to tell her that you'll be arriving a week after me and you've promised to pay for the both of us."

"No chance Dusty, she loves me 'no shit'. Anyway, you'll be too busy buying all the old mamasans a drink. Damn I miss that place. Just remember not to bring back anything that you can't put in a suitcase."

It was a pain that they couldn't take their R&R in pairs but that would have left too high a workload for those left behind.

While Dusty was away living the high life in the bars of Wanchai and Kowloon, work continued at a steady pace.

The night after he left, Da Nang was the target of a major rocket offensive by the VC. Their major target was the Da Nang airfield but with their primitive aiming devices, 122mm and 140mm rockets were landing all over the city. They knew it was going to be a long night as some would certainly have dud fired. And that meant an EOD team would have to deal with it.

Once the attack had begun to die away, the radio came to life, requesting their assistance in a half a dozen places at the same time.

They spent the reminder of the night answering calls for EOD assistance as a number of the rockets had in fact failed to detonate on impact. One rocket had scored a direct hit on a USAF C-130 parked on the ramp at Da Nang airfield. The port wing had been severed by the blast and the aircraft had burned almost beyond recognition.

A number of civilian homes around Da Nang had also been demolished with the death toll close to 30 - mostly innocent civilians.

After Dusty arrived back from leave, John thought it a good idea for the remainder of the Team to cycle through their R&R at this time and get it out of the way. Stan went next. Being a newlywed, he headed home to see his bride in Sydney. The Chief followed, also to Sydney. Bit hard to explain to the wife and kids why you took leave in the hotspots of Asia instead of coming home. Pete opted for Taipei and Willy decided on Bangkok.

They both had very memorable R&Rs and they both managed to fall in love several times, although Pete's love life seemed to cost him a lot more cash than Willy's did. He suspected Pete partied harder and he certainly didn't mind sharing his wealth with the bar girls.

Bangkok was as Willy remembered it. Great food, endless bars, lots of pretty girls and outstanding beer. He just wandered from bar to bar, chatting to the prettiest of the girls, buying them the occasional drink and eating at odd hours, whenever he felt the need.

Sometimes he would chat to the girls until the early hours of the morning, just enjoying their company and talking to them. Sometimes he would take one that he fancied back to his hotel for the night, sometimes he would go home alone.

It felt very strange to be in a city where there were no uniforms, no helicopters buzzing overhead, no rifle fire and no need to look over your shoulder all the time.

Just as he had started to really relax, kick back and begin to enjoy himself, it was time to get the bus to the airport for the flight back to Saigon. Willy thought it bizarre to be leaving this lively bustling city knowing he was heading back to a land completely ravaged by war. He found the contrast to be a little unsettling.

Pete came back from Taipei a complete wreck, and completely broke. He had met up with a Navy SEAL he knew on the flight over and they didn't stop partying for 5 days. John declined his R&R feeling that as the OIC, he should remain with his team at all times.

All of them had settled comfortably into their roles as members of an operational EOD team. Being in a war zone had become almost *'normal'* for them. They were now very experienced and it felt as if they had been doing this all their working lives. Nothing else mattered other than doing their job as safely and professionally as possible.

Being called out at any hour of the day or night was as natural as eating or sleeping.

Their professional training and instincts had taken over their every response, their every action. They trusted each other implicitly without ever being mindful of it, or at least thinking about it. Their adrenalin levels were always high, their senses were on full alert without consciously having to switch them on or off.

They had molded into pretty much a six man machine.

And then out of the wild blue, came a

sledgehammer blow that knocked them all for six.

The Chief had flown up to Cua Viet near the DMZ to assess an EOD salvage operation in the Cua Viet river. He had scrounged a ride north on a milk run aboard a Marine Huey and had been gone for a couple of days.

The remainder of the Team were all in the hooch having a quiet beer when John received a phone call. An Army Bell 206 Jet Ranger (Kiowa) returning to Da Nang from Cua Viet earlier that afternoon had taken heavy small arms and RPG fire while crossing the Hai Van Pass to the north of Da Nang.

Witnesses had reported seeing the chopper spinning out of control with most likely a catastrophic gearbox failure and it had crashed heavily into the steep hillside. Both the pilot and passenger had been killed on impact.

They were quite certain it was the Aussie Chief who was the passenger and they had asked John to identify the body.

When John told his men, there was a deathly silence in the hooch.

Stan was the only one who could muster any words and all he could say was *"Jesus Christ – not Harry."*

They all just sat there for the best part of five minutes, each trying to come to grips with the fact that they had lost their Chief. He was the *'Chief'*. He was the lynch pin of the team. Fifteen years in the CD Branch. One of the most respected men they had. His loss was beyond belief – not the Chief. He was indestructible.

Finally John stood up. He was pale and looked like he had aged ten years.

"Righto, better get on with it I suppose. I'll call Operations and ask that all routine calls be tasked to Army EOD for the remainder of the night. I'll be back in an hour or two. You blokes be right?"

Stan said quietly, *"I'll come with you Boss. You don't need this on your own."*

Willy said, *"We'll be right Boss."*

After John and Stan had left, the remaining three sailors sat in stunned disbelief. No one said a word. What could they say. They each had to confront their own feelings and thoughts and sort through them before they could say anything.

When Willy eventually looked up at Dusty and Pete, they were both looking at him. Being the more senior AB, he felt they were waiting for him to say something. OK, they couldn't sit there all night feeling sorry for themselves. Willy said,

"Don't know about you blokes, but I need a fuckin' good shot of Bourbon."

They followed him into the bar where he poured three decent slugs of Old Grandad bourbon whiskey. With a tear in his eye he raised his glass and said,

"Here's to Harry. The best goddamn Chief in the Navy."

Pete and Dusty both quietly echoed, *"To the Chief."*

After knocking down the first shot, Willy refilled the three glasses. Pete stared intently at the dark liquid and said,

"Fuckin' unbelievable. One minute he's here, and then

he's gone. Just like that."

Dusty, also staring at his glass as if it might bring the Chief back, said,

"It sort of brings it home doesn't it? We're in a goddamn war zone. It could have been any one of us."

Willy realized it was best for them to keep talking. They had to come to grips with their shock and grief very quickly.

The war wasn't going to stop, and their responsibilities weren't going to be put on hold while they adjusted to this loss of their fatherly mentor and mate.

They belted down the second shot and Willy said,

"Let's have a cup of coffee and wait for the Boss and Stan. Last thing they want to see is us half shit-faced when they get back."

The three of them settled in the kitchen drinking brewed American coffee. Their conversation turned to speculation as to what would happen next. How it would affect the operation of the team, how they would get him home, how Canberra would handle a replacement for the Chief. They were a six man unit and it would be extremely difficult to operate a man short for any length of time.

They heard the Jeep pull up outside and waited. John and Stan walked through the door both looking far older than their years.

John confirmed the worst,

"It was the Chief in the chopper. It happened just as they said. Both dead on impact. At least it was quick. I'm

going to have a large whiskey and then write a few signals. Suggest you fellas try to get the head down. See you in the morning and we'll talk about where we go from here over breakfast."

It was a very gloomy crew who sat around the table next morning. They had all awakened wondering if it was a bad dream. The looks on their faces showed it had been no dream.

John, who obviously hadn't slept a wink, said

"I've had a number of signals over the past few hours from Canberra. Here's the deal. Plans are underway to get the Chief home within the next few days. Stan is going to escort him home and will stay long enough to represent all of us at a full Military funeral in Sydney. There will be a memorial service this afternoon at 1300 in the base chapel. We will wear full Aussie greens. Regarding a replacement, Canberra has agreed with my recommendations. As of this moment, Stan is on higher duties allowance for Chief and will take over as Chief of the Team. Willy will take on the role of Team Leading Hand supporting Stan. Our standby, Matt, has been told to pack his bags and will be coming back to Saigon with Stan. Things will be a bit tight for the next week but I know you blokes can handle it. We have a job to do and the Chief would want and expect us to get on with it. If anyone has anything to say or any questions, let's get it out of the way now."

They all just shook their heads. There was nothing left to be said. John stood,

"After the service, it will be business as usual. Me and Dusty, Willy and Pete. 24 on, 24 off. Thanks fellas, and keep your heads up."

CHAPTER 13

Ten days later, Willy picked up Stan and Matt at the *'Air America'* pad (a private airline owned and operated by the CIA) at Da Nang airfield. It was good to have Stan back and good to see Matt again.

It was obvious Matt was pretty excited to be there albeit aware of the sad circumstances responsible for his being in Vietnam. On the drive back to the hooch, Stan told Willy about the funeral and the reaction at home to the Chief's death. They had given him a traditional Divers send off.

Over a few beers that evening, the Team closed the door at least temporarily on the loss of their Chief. John gave Matt a brief on the primary responsibilities of the team, examples of recent operations and what their standard operating procedures were.

He was to be given a condensed introduction to Vietnam by going out on every job for the following two weeks. Matt was to watch closely and follow the instructions of whichever team member he was working with. He would be gradually assimilated into the Team.

All took turns as time permitted to show Matt around Da Nang. He was introduced to the more mundane duties such as picking up the mail and stores. He met their US contacts on base and he was taken to the firing range and demolition range to bring him up to speed on how the Team did things.

Being in a war zone, he soon learnt not all was done by the book. Matt quickly adapted and they all knew he was going to be OK. He hadn't been part of their early indoctrination and hadn't yet seen a shot fired in anger but his team mates were all comfortable that he would not let them down when the shit hit the fan.

It was bizarre what a few months in Vietnam had done to these young men. They all felt years older than Matt yet he was in fact the oldest of the AB's.

During his first week in country, the team responded to a few false alarms at Deep Water piers and in their spare time resumed the recovery operation of the ordnance thrown out from the ammunition barge in Da Nang harbour. The false alarms were common. Nervous sentries would see flotsam near a vessel and assume the worst. Often they would open fire on anything they thought suspicious and if it happened at night, they would often report sighting swimmers near a vessel.

Of course every call was assumed to be the real thing. No one could afford to relax their vigilance.

Matt had his first real taste of the more serious end of the business when they were asked to check out two Navy vehicles which had been parked in a supposedly secure compound. There was some evidence of a forced entry to the locked enclosure so it was assumed the vehicles may have been tampered with. With Matt taking the lead, they soon discovered both vehicles had in fact been booby trapped. A slab of US manufacture plastic explosives had been attached to the firewall of each truck with an electric detonator wired into the ignition switch. After cutting the blasting cap's thin leads and removing the explosive material a thorough search for other possible devices was carried out.

The new man had been blooded.

Several days later a call came in requesting the team to check out a 500 pound bomb which had been found by a rice farmer while ploughing his rice paddy in preparation for planting near the village of Ha Loc, to the west of Da Nang. The area had been bombed during the earliest days of US involvement and if the report was correct, it sounded like a dud which had been sitting quietly for a number of years in the farmer's rice paddy.

After a 25 minute chopper ride, John and two of the boys landed on the outskirts of the village. An ARVN officer and interpreter were waiting for them.

As it turned out, the bomb had a *'hung'* striker mechanism. John discussed the available options with Willy and Dusty. They all agreed that physically relocating it to a safe area for disposal was not an option so decided the best alternative was to explosively disarm the bomb *'in situ'*. That meant firing a small specialised explosive device on the nose of the bomb case which, in theory, should totally destroy the actuating mechanism before it initiated the main explosive filling. However, if the charge was not set correctly, it could open the case and set off the explosive filler at *low order*; still a big bang, however much less catastrophic than the bomb detonating as intended by the manufacturer at *high order*. It was a risk but it was their only real choice.

Several farmers' huts were very close by and the village was well within the danger zone should the worst case scenario occur.

John made the decision – they would attempt to disarm it with a linear shaped charge. The village chief was told what they intended to do and that he should move everyone in the village out to a safe distance in preparation for the worst case.

While Willy and Dusty prepared the small C-4 explosive charge, John accompanied the village chief and interpreter to ensure that the village was in fact cleared of all people, ducks, chickens, children, dogs and water buffalo out to a safe distance.

When John returned he told the lads that the chief was very anxious about possible damage to his village as he had seen the devastation that a 500 lb bomb could inflict on huts and he could not understand the concept of a partial detonation. John said with a grin,

"If the bastard high orders, we'd better be ready to get the hell out of Dodge real quick."

He wasn't really worried as they had carried out this same procedure on many occasions. However there was always the one that went wrong.

Willy and Dusty positioned the charge on the bomb and with the nod from John, initiated the time fuse. Once they saw smoke issuing in a steady stream from the end of the fuse, Willy called *"Fire in the hole"* and they all walked back to the main track and headed for cover.

Ten minutes later they heard a sharp crack as about a quarter stick of C-4 detonated. They all looked at each other and broke into smiles. The main charge had not initiated and with a bit of luck the nose fuse was totally destroyed.

They waited 10 minutes before wandering back to the 500 pounder. It had worked perfectly. The bomb was now harmless enough to be airlifted by chopper to a safe location for disposal.

When the chief was told that his village was now safe, he was ecstatic and would not stop grinning and shaking their hands. Dusty smiled and said to no-one in particular,

"Another day, another dollar."

John replied, *"Well done lads. Let's go home."*

In the Jeep on the way back to the chopper Dusty reflected, *"You know Boss, there are plenty of things about this goddamn war that suck, but a job like that makes you feel good. Handled by the wrong people, that 500 pounder could have destroyed that vill and every living thing in it. I'm feelin' alright."*

John reflected for a moment,

"You're right Dusty. Makes your day. I think I'm ready for a cold beer and a good cigar."

Several days later the Boss said he wanted

three of the Team to spend about a week at Cua Viet, just south of the DMZ. They were to drive up, taking their diving gear and an air compressor with them.

A landing craft had hit a mine and sunk in approximately 15 feet of water only about 16 klicks upstream from the US Navy compound. The CDs had been asked if they could recover and dispose of the ordnance and ammunition loaded in her well deck.

John told Stan he would be taking Matt and Willy. Matt hadn't been out of Da Nang so it would be an eye opener for him. The drive north along Highway One would take them through Phu Bai, where they would spend the night in an Army compound, then on to Hue, the home of the Vietnamese Emperors and the ancient capital of Vietnam.

They would cross the Perfume River and skirt what remained of the ancient citadel (*it had been mostly destroyed during the Communist offensive of Tet '68*) before heading to the Provincial capital of Quang Tri.

From there it was a muddy track winding through rice paddies and villages before they hit the sandy coastal expanse of Cua Viet. In Vietnamese, 'Cua' (*pronounced Quaa*) means bay, or river mouth.

Cua Viet was situated at the mouth of the Dong Ha River. It was the most northerly US compound before South Vietnam became North Vietnam. US Military vessels plied the river carrying a variety of military cargo from Dong Ha to Cua Viet.

The drive to Phu Bai in normal times would have been a very picturesque trip. Crossing the Hai Van pass was spectacular. Looking behind them as they climbed the twisting road to the top of the Pass, they had a superb view of Da Nang harbour, Da Nang city and the coastal strip all the way south to Marble Mountain.

Phu Bai was a very active US Army base with troops and vehicles constantly on the move and a busy airfield. An early start the following morning ensured they would be able to arrive at Cua Viet by mid afternoon. The sailors had no intention of being on the dirt track beyond Quang Tri after sundown. Travel in broad daylight was risky enough.

The track wound through rice paddies and clumps of natural bamboo which were perfect spots to ambush a lone vehicle.

Cua Viet was a small outpost with a mixture of Vietnamese Military and US Navy personnel. On Willy's first trip to the tiny base a few months earlier, he had been taken aback by the number of Navy patrol boats, or the remains of Navy patrol boats which littered the beach along the sandy foreshore. These were vessels which had fallen prey to the VC. All had been damaged by river mines or by rocket fire.

Much to Matt's surprise, the EOD hooch which was the living quarters for the two US EOD advisors based there, was nothing more than a flat topped barge which had been dragged up onto the beach with a makeshift hut on the upper deck. This was their home. The barge was tilted at a permanent 5 degree angle because of the slope of the beach and consequently everything inside the EOD quarters from bunks to chairs and tables were on a considerable list to starboard. Within 10 metres of the barge was a sandbagged mortar pit which Matt was soon to discover became quite active at various hours during the night, especially just as he was nodding off to sleep.

Twenty metres further on was the *'Monkey cage'*. This was the South Vietnamese version of *'cells'*. It consisted of a rough timber floor about 4 feet square with sides of barbed wire and was topped by a sheet of galvanized iron to keep the worst of the sun off the offender during the heat of the day and the rain during the night. The wrongdoer could spend a night or up to a week in the cage, depending on the severity of his sentence.

After a very simple meal in the mess hall, the troops headed back to the EOD hooch. Much to Matt's surprise, Lee, a Chief and the senior US advisor, pulled out a 40 ounce bottle of Seagrams VO whiskey and poured everyone a stiff shot. He then dug into a reefer (refrigerator) and pulled out several cans of Coke and Pabst Blue Ribbon beer.

Willy saw the surprised look on Matt's face and with a grin said quietly,
"Welcome to Vietnam Mate."

The landing craft slipped its moorings just as the diffused glow of first light began to expose the wispy mist hanging over the calm brown river like a damp veil. The coxswain headed into mid channel and advanced the throttles while the crew took up their positions on the 60mm mortar, M60 and .50 cal machine guns.

As Lee had suggested the previous evening, the EOD team were loaded for *'bear'* and they put one *'up the spout'* of their weapons and found some cover for the short ride up river. They all had M16s but Willy had learnt a valuable lesson from his mate Pete and also carried an M79 grenade launcher with plenty of spare 40mm HE rounds.

The fog would work in their favour for a while as the banks of the river were still barely visible. If Charlie was lying in wait, they would, with luck, be swallowed by the mist before Charlie could react to their passing.

The downside was that there would be no air support available if *'the shit hit the fan'*. At least not until the fog had lifted.

They were no more than 15 minutes out of Cua Viet when a prolonged burst of automatic fire erupted from the thick vegetation lining the river bank on their starboard side.

Every weapon on board the landing craft returned fire as one.

Thirty seconds later and it was over. The thick fog had reclaimed the boat and the VC had lost sight of them.

Stan's first instinct was to check that Willy and Matt were OK. Matt had a wild look in his eyes. It was the first time someone had tried to kill him and he was wound up like a spring.

Willy just raised his eyebrows at him as if to say, *'Here we go again'*.

Lee immediately checked on the boat crew. All gave him the thumbs up except the sailor manning the .50 caliber machine gun. He was slumped behind his weapon. Lee and Stan both scrambled over to him, but it was clear there was no need to hurry. A bullet had torn half his throat away.

After a quick head count it was confirmed the machine gunner was the only casualty from the brief encounter. Stan helped Lee gently move the sailor's body into the cabin where they covered him with a poncho liner. Lee then went to the wheelhouse to give the boat Chief a *'sitrep'* and radio Cua Viet to advise of the contact and discuss their next move.

Stan moved back to the .50 cal ensuring it was loaded and ready to go.

The only sound was the steady hum of the boat's diesels. Five minutes later, Lee slid alongside Stan,

"The boat skipper and I have been in contact with Cua Viet. They have advised that a chopper passing over the wreck site has spotted a number of possible VC in the vicinity so more than likely, we will have another welcoming committee. They have requested 2 Snakes from the Air Cav at Phu Bai to recce the area and try to sort the bastards out before we get there. If it's too hot, we are to standby for a possible insertion of ARVN troops to secure the area for us. Once that is completed a Dust-off will come by and pick up our KIA."

Stan replied,

"Righto Lee, I'll get my blokes to back up the crew weapons as there's a good chance the shit will hit the fan again before we get onsite."

"Roger that," said Lee, *"I'll stay close to the radio."*

The curtain of mist hanging over the river was lifting and visibility was improving the further they got upstream. That meant they could see the river banks quite clearly now as they slid by.

It also meant Charlie could see them more clearly as well.

The boat Chief eased his throttles forward, increasing engine revolutions to maximum as the fog thinned and the boat continued to head up river. Without needing to be told, everybody onboard was intently scanning every inch of the riverbank for any possible sign of the enemy.

Matt leaned towards Willy and asked,

"How the fuck do we dive on this tub if Charlie is shooting at us?"

Willy shifted his gaze from the riverbank,

"We play it by ear when we get there Mate. Not much else we can do."

About 20 minutes further upstream, with the mist gone and the temperature rising, they were all beginning to sweat a great deal in their heavy flak jackets. Willy had the feeling it was going to be a long day.

Without warning, from upriver they saw a number of flashes followed by a large fireball and as they watched, it developed into a rising mushroom shaped cloud. In what seemed an eternity but was in fact only about 5 seconds, the sounds of the blasts swept over them. Matt was the first to ask what they were all thinking,

"Christ, what was that?"

Willy, after a moment's hesitation, replied as the engines came back to idle and the boat began to lose way,

"I reckon that was our barge."

Lee was coming down from the wheelhouse towards Stan.

"Just had a sitrep from that chopper which was overflying the wreck. He stuck around and decided to call in a couple of 'fast movers' (Air Force F-4 Phantoms) who were in the area, instead of waiting for the Snakes to arrive. They dumped a load of 500lb low drags around the wreck site to sort out Charlie but appears one landed in the well deck of the barge and the whole lot cooked off. We no longer have a job to do."

"Shit hot." replied Stan. *"Let's get the fuck out of here."*

"Roger that. We're not here."

Lee headed back to the wheelhouse to tell the 1st class Bosun's Mate to turn the boat around and head back to Cua Viet.

Willy and Matt were near enough to hear what Lee had said. Stan added,

"We're going back but we're not out of the woods yet so keep your eyes open. Charlie is probably still parked downriver somewhere waiting for another crack at us."

Much to their surprise they covered the 35 minute journey downstream to Cua Viet without any further contact.

Once they had unloaded their equipment from the boat, Lee took them up to see the Skipper of the Base to give their report.

As they strolled back to the EOD hooch, Lee grinned and said,

"What do you boys think about barbecued ribs, potato salad and cold beer on the beach at 1600?"

"Sounds alright to me Chief." replied Stan.

Matt was shaking his head as he looked across to Willy and said in a subdued tone,

"This joint is unbelievable. One minute some bastard is trying to shoot the shit out of us and the next minute we're going to have a barbeque on the beach as if the war was a thousand miles away."

Willy grinned,

"You'll get used to it Mate. Things could be worse. You could be back in Australia putting up with all the protesting soft cocks, the potheads and the political bullshit."

Later that afternoon, relaxing on the beach drinking their fourth beer and having just eaten the best ribs they had ever tasted, Willy and Matt were both in reflective moods.

Lee and Stan were sitting around the beer cooler bull-shitting about which country made the best beer. Willy realised that Matt was trying to get his thoughts in order about what had happened that day and he had no intention of interrupting him. It was important that Matt handled it in his own way. Willy had been there himself.

Finally Matt broke the silence,

"You know mate, I'm having trouble getting my head

around this shit. Look at us. Sitting on a beach watching a spectacular sunset over those mountains. Just had a great feed and we've got heaps of cold beer. This is a remarkable country. I love being around you blokes and these Yanks are good hands, but today some bastard tried to kill us and I saw that young bloke get blown away. You've been here longer than me. How the fuck do you handle this? How do you get used to it?"

Willy took his time in replying.

"Matt, everyone has to deal with this in his own way. This country plays with your head but let me tell you, you've got to get on top of it real quick. Unfortunately we are not particularly welcome here. Along with the Americans, we are seen by the Vietnamese as just one more foreign invader supporting an unpopular and extremely corrupt government. So we just do our job – to the best of our ability."

They both sat quietly, sipping their beers and watching the gentle ripples wash over the sand.

Willy, trying to get his own thoughts in order, continued,

"You know mate, we all saw that bloke die today, and it could have been any one of us, but it wasn't. I reckon you have to believe that you're a bit bulletproof just to keep getting out of bed every morning. That's not to say that you don't expect the worst and try to be ready for it, but you can't let emotions play with your mind. It's funny how impersonal death can become if you don't know the bloke, like today. When we lost the Chief, none of us knew how to deal with it. We didn't know what to do next. But you know what, it doesn't take long to remember where you are. There's no time here to mourn

anyone. Maybe there will be a time for it later, after we get home – I don't really know. You just have to put it aside or it'll tear you apart. If your mind isn't on the job every waking moment, you're not going to survive this joint."

Willy paused, deep in thought.

"You know, I sometimes wonder about what it's going to be like going home. I find it hard to imagine living a normal life again. This place gets to you. I might even be addicted to it in some ways. I mean, every day here you're on an adrenaline high, your nerves are tingling, you have no idea what the next minute, hour or day is going to bring. You're living on a knife edge, but you know something, I've never felt so alive. Know what I mean? Our lives will never be the same again after being in this country. And you know what, no-one at home is going to be able to understand or even give a shit about what has happened to us up here. I have seen big changes in the rest of the team. They're not the same blokes I came up here with. I love them like brothers because of what we're been through together, but they've changed, I've changed. We'll never turn back the clock Mate."

There was long silence between them as Matt pondered Willy's words.

Finally he said,

"Yeah, I reckon you're right. Thanks mate, that helps a lot."

'EOD Hooch' - Cua Viet.

Remains of mined boats at Cua Viet.

Mined vessel at Cua Viet.
'Birdcage' in foreground.

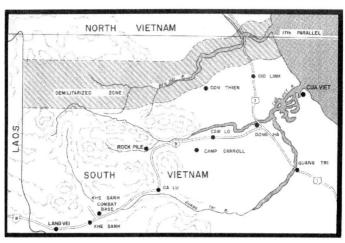

Cua Viet and the DMZ.

CHAPTER 14

When they arrived back in Da Nang, John was waiting for them. Stan filled him in on the details of the op as he did with every job conducted by the team. It had to written up in the monthly Report of Proceedings which were sent to Navy Office back in Canberra.

"Righto, you might all want a hot tubs and catch up on a bit of sleep," John broke into a smile, *"but first I've got some good news for you Willy. While you were in Cua Viet, I received advice that the US system has put you and Pete up for bravery awards for pulling that US advisor out on Can Thanh island. You and Pete have both been nominated for the Silver Star by the Americans. Your recommendation states you both 'displayed personal courage of the highest order under fire and in the face of the enemy, above and beyond the call of duty'. Congratulations and well done. Not sure yet if the shiny bums in Canberra will allow us to accept American awards but I'll be pushing my hardest."*

As John shook Willy's hand, he grinned

"And it's your shout."

"Well done boys." said Stan as he put his arms around Willy and Pete's shoulders and then shook both their hands. *"You both deserve it big time, and I'll enjoy drinking a free beer tonight. Be the first one*

either of you've ever bought me."

So that night the team kicked back and had a few beers in recognition of Willy's and Pete's unexpected nomination for Silver Stars. John and Matt stuck to the soft drinks as they had the duty. After John had said a few words about the significance of their gallantry awards, he said with some emotion that they were both a credit to Australia, the Navy and the CD branch.

Pete raised his beer and said,

"Thanks Boss. I'm just glad that I'm here with you blokes at my back. Cheers."

They drained their beers and Willy pulled out some fresh ones from the reefer (*refrigerator*). He then lifted his can and said what he knew they were all thinking,

"There's one bloke missing tonight who would have made it pretty special. Here's to the Chief. The best of the best."

After they had all raised their beers to their Chief, the Boss quietly reminded them,

"OK fellas, tomorrow is another day and we've still got a very important job to do. I don't have to tell you to keep your eye on the ball and to stay focused. I want us all to go home together. See you in the morning."

The Boss then left them to it, very conscious that they all deserved and needed to have a few quiet beers together. He was fully aware of the mental strain his boys were under and a few beers was the only way that he knew they could help ease it.

It was a night for a few quiet drinks amongst

mates who were coming to an understanding that a very special yet unspoken bond had developed between them all. It was as if they had been together forever.

They understood each other better than brothers ever could. They were a *'band of brothers'* in every sense of the word.

Stan kept the conversation light hearted. He knew when their spirits needed a boost. To him, these young men were his family. Certainly at that moment in time, his only family, and he was determined to do everything within his power to look after them. They were his boys and he knew they counted on him. He would not let them down – not under any circumstances.

Da Nang was often called *'Rocket city'* because the airfield was a favourite target of the VC for their 122mm and 140mm rocket attacks and the divers regularly heard distant explosions from the incoming rockets. Living on the Tourane peninsular fortunately had the diver's location beyond the range of the rockets.

During the Team's third week in country, they had experienced their first serious rocket attack on the Da Nang Air Base. Over 40 122mm and 140mm rockets had landed in and around the airfield. They were fired electrically from tube launchers which were easily and quickly transported, aimed, fired and moved again. The Russian-made 122mm rocket, was lighter, more accurate and had a longer range than its 140mm cousin – approximately 10,000 meters as against 8,800 meters. However the 140mm contained about 10 pounds of HE and inflicted considerably more damage.

The problem for the defenders was how to return fire as the VC invariably launched from close proximity to villages which made it difficult to return effective suppressing fire without inflicting civilian casualties. But in this case, within several minutes, US artillery units had plotted the launch site locations and selective counter battery fire was underway.

Within another few minutes an Air Force AC-47 on air alert (nicknamed *Puff the Magic Dragon*) was circling the suspected launching sites looking for targets to attack. '*Spooky*' as it was also known, was armed with three 7.62mm miniguns which could selectively fire either 50 or 100 rounds per second. Cruising in an overhead left-hand orbit at 120 knots and an altitude of 3,000 ft, the old DC-3 gunship could put a bullet into every square yard of a football field-sized target in three seconds. As long as its 45 flare and 24,000-round basic load of ammunition held out, it could do this intermittently while loitering over a target for hours.

With *Spooky* in the area, the VC couldn't get out of there fast enough.

The rockets were being launched from an area near Hoa Hung Village, six miles southwest of Da Nang. It was later found there had been five separate firing sites, each with up to four individual launchers.

At the airfield that night, 5 USAF airmen had been killed with 58 wounded and 2 Marines killed with 21 wounded. Materiel damage was considerable. The Marines lost an F-8 Crusader with a second F-8 badly damaged. The Air Force lost a C-130 Hercules from a direct hit on the port wing and two F-4 Phantoms were completely wasted. Several other aircraft were also badly damaged.

In addition, the incoming VC rockets had destroyed an NCO's barracks and a fuel dump with considerable damage done to the runways, taxiways and several other buildings. A very successful night for Victor Charlie.

Not all the rockets had detonated so the Divers were called out to help deal with any unexploded rockets found outside the airfield perimeter. Everything inside the perimeter was dealt with by Marine & Air Force EOD personnel as it was their home turf.

Just another day, another dollar.

CHAPTER 15

One quiet morning, with Mama San cooking a dish of fried rice for Willy and Dusty's breakfast, liberally laced with fish sauce, John received a phone call from the OIC of the SEAL team which operated out of the nearby Special Forces camp. Stan was bitching about the fishy smell wafting through the kitchen from the pungent Nuoc Mam when John came into the kitchen with a grin and said,

"Damn that smells good. Is that all for you Stan or can I have some?"

"Boss, you can have all you fucking like. You won't catch me eating that shit."

John laughed,

"Yeh, my system is not quite up to it this time of morning either but you're gonna hurt Mamasan's feelings. Look at her, she's pouting already. Anyway, back to business. After breakfast you and I have a meeting with the SEAL team at 09 hundred. Lt Polanski has a job coming up and he wants to discuss our possible involvement. From what he said, might need two or three of us."

"Sounds like another walk in the park." grinned Dusty.

Lt. JG Darryl Polanski was the head honcho of the SEAL platoon operating in I Corps at that time.

He was on his second tour and according to his troops, he had his *'shit together'*. His platoon of *'frogs'* had visited the Aussie hooch on a number of occasions and they had all gotten half wasted together as well as doing the occasional joint recce of some of the more infamous red light establishments in downtown Da Nang.

On one such trip, the Military police had chosen to raid a particular business establishment whilst Willy, Dusty and two of the SEALs were relaxing and having a quiet beer while chatting to the ladies. Being fit young men, and wanting to avoid a confrontation with the Army *'Gestapo'*, they bolted out the back door before the MPs had time to react.

Willy later told Pete and Stan that they ran headlong for about 150 metres in the dark before they all went ass over head into rolls of coiled barbed wire. The four of them still had the scars to prove it.

A mutual respect, both personal and professionally, had already developed between the two group of sailors. They had each other's measure.

Lt Polanski and his Chief were waiting for them when they arrived. When everyone had a fresh coffee in their hand, Lt 'Ski' got down to business.

"Thanks for coming John - Chief. We have recently received some pretty solid Intel about the movement and caching of substantial amounts of weapons, ammunition, money and documents coming down from

the North. It is being carried across the DMZ at night and then being transferred down the Dong Ha river. Our Intel people say it is being cached very close to a couple of deserted huts about 10 clicks west of Dong Ha. Intel believes the next delivery is due two nights from tonight and we have been tasked to destroy the cache, take out the delivery boys and bring back a couple of live ones for interrogation if possible. We understand that the cache is considerable and that's where you guys come in. The mission is to completely destroy everything with the exception of the documents and cash. You guys are good at what you do and we're good at what we do, so we'd like you to come along. While you're doing your thing, we'll be doing our thing and covering your asses at the same time. Being Aussie Navy, we can only request you to take part in the op. We would like to have at least two of your guys John. I'll be taking the team in and Chief Dalton here will be along as well. We're planning an insertion by chopper and skimmer and then quietly hoofing it for the last several clicks to the target. Three Army Hueys and a gunship will be standing by to extract the team - a hot extraction if necessary. We'll be back in Phu Bai for breakfast."

Ski smiled, had a mouthful of cold coffee and looked the Aussie officer straight in the eye,

"Questions?"

Stan looked sideways at John with his usual shit grin on his face. John knew it was his call but Stan's smile let him know he was comfortable with their participation in the op.

John nodded and said,

"We're in Ski." He turned to Stan and said, *"Who do*

you want to take Chief?"

"I'll take Willy and Pete if it's three, or just Willy if it's two. From what's been said, two is enough – we don't want to be getting in each other's way."

Ski put his coffee cup back on the table and said,

"Thanks for your help John. We're happy to have your guys along. We know you can look after yourselves." Turning to Stan, *"Chief, if you and Willy could be here tomorrow at 1000, we'll walk through the op-plan in detail and later in the afternoon we'll all head out to the range to test fire our weapons. Weapons are personal choice. The following afternoon we'll transit by chopper to Dong Ha to prepare for our insertion that night. Don't have to tell you guys that this is 'eyes and ears only'. I'll owe you a few beers when we get back. Thanks again."*

On the drive back to their hooch, John said,

"I know I don't have to say it Stan, but just keep in mind that these blokes play fair dinkum. This is a heavy duty op and it could all turn to custard pretty quickly, so just be ready for any eventuality, OK? I want you blokes back in one piece."

"No worries Boss. Willy's as solid as a rock, and these crazy assed SEALS have got their 'shit in one bag'. Couldn't be in better company if we tried."

Many SEALs chose to carry the 5.56mm Stoner 63 light machine gun. It was relatively light (*about half the weight of the M60 7.62mm machine gun which was used by the rest of the Military*), had a drum magazine with 150 rounds and could fire up to 1,000 rounds per minute.

Stan and Willy would each be carrying 30 pounds of C-4 plastic explosives plus the detonating cord and blasting caps required to hook it all up. They both chose to carry the Car 15 rifle with six 25 round mags and a Colt .45 with four 7 round mags on their belts as close quarter weapons and of course their trusty K bar knives attached to their shoulder webbing.

On the range the following day both the Aussies were again awestruck by the amount of firepower the SEALs could lay down on a target with their Stoners.

After everyone had sighted their weapons, Willy quietly said to Stan,

"If the shit hits the fan, we've got the right blokes on our side."

At 1600 the next day, they were all waiting patiently at the chopper pad for the three Army Helos which were to transport them to their initial staging point at Dong Ha. The SEAL Chief had completed the first of his checks of all equipment and weapons. All was in order and they were ready to go.

As the familiar sound of the approaching Hueys grew in intensity, Willy looked sideways at Stan and said quietly with a grin stretched across his face,

"Where I am going, I know not where, when I will get there, I am uncertain, all I know is I am on my way…."

Stan smiled,

"You've been watching too many movies. Wasn't that in that flick we watched the other night – 'Paint your

wagon'?"

"That's the one – good movie."

"Well Mate, this ain't a fuckin movie – I'm more concerned about getting back than where we're going!!"

"Roger that." replied Willy. The grin had disappeared – time for business.

They all finished a quick light meal at the Marine base, avoiding the inquisitive looks from the soldiers in the chow hall. The team were dressed in a mixture of not so clean cammies and Levis and wore no rank or unit insignia. Their boots hadn't seen polish for a very long time and in fact, some of them wore running shoes.

Many of the Marines had never seen SEALs before and they were very curious about these tough looking and serious faced men who appeared so contemptuous of normal Military dress codes. All who saw them however, knew better than to ask any questions or pass any comment.

Back in a small hut near the airfield, Ski and the SEAL Chief, Dalton, went through the final briefing while the team applied cam cream to each other and double checked their personal weapons and equipment.

The Helos were ready and standing by to airlift them to a location where they would board skimmers for the final leg to their drop-off point. From there they would make a tactical approach to the huts and set up an ambush, to lie in wait for the planned delivery to take place.

After inserting the SEAL team the choppers

would fly back to the Dong Ha Marine Base via a dog-leg route, carefully avoiding the target area, where they would refuel and wait for the call to extract the team.

One of the SEAL platoon members was an LDNN (*Vietnamese Navy version of a US SEAL*). He was familiar with the area and would lead the Team in. Ski had assured the Aussies that this guy was a damn good operator and had proven in past ops to be very reliable.

The timings should have the Team in ambush positions on the ground by 0300. Plenty of time before the expected delivery was due to take place just prior to first light. The moon was in its *'waning crescent'* so the available light would be near perfect for their planned insertion and movement to the target area.

Once on the ground, Stan and Willy would position themselves in the 14 man SEAL platoon immediately behind Ski. If the shit hit the fan on the way in, they were to stick close to Ski. The LDNN was to take point and the SEAL Chief would be directly behind Willy.

A high priority was placed on looking after the EOD men and their explosives.

The choppers dropped the team onto a secure LZ near the river and the skimmers were waiting. Willy and Stan loaded into different boats so as to split the explosives. The boat coxswains with their starlight night vision moved slowly into mid stream and headed downriver with everyone on full alert, prepared for any unforeseen event.

The trip downstream proved uneventful and they were at the drop-off point right on schedule. The boats turned in and softly nudged into the river bank. Not a word was spoken as the *'men with green faces'* slipped ashore and quietly set up a defensive perimeter. The skimmers then slowly and carefully backed out into the river, turned upstream and were soon out of sight.

Silence returned to the area. The SEAL team waited for the night insects to resume their busy chatter. Only then did Ski give the signal to move out.

One at a time they formed up and without a sound, moved out in single file.

They moved stealthily, like the shadows they had become, alongside what appeared to be the remnants of a long disused track. At what seemed to be erratic intervals, the entire patrol stopped as one and just listened, not moving and not making a sound. The SEAL who was acting as *'tail end charlie'* was particularly watchful for anyone coming from their rear.

During these stops, it occurred to Willy how finely tuned his senses had become. He could hear every little sound, he could see and feel and smell his surroundings as if they were a part of him.

About two and a half hours after they had left the riverbank, a hand signal was passed back down the line to halt. Everyone vanished into the scrub off the track, alternating, one to the left, one to the right. Each man positioning himself to cover his own outward facing defensive arc of fire.

The SEAL Chief quietly moved forward to remain at the sharp end until the two point men, including the Vietnamese LDNN returned from a recce of the planned ambush position.

After an hour the signal came back for Ski to move forward. He indicated to Stan and Willy to follow. Other than the night insects, they had not heard a sound since they had come to a halt.

The two point men and Chief Dalton were waiting. In a quiet whisper, the point SEAL advised there were five VC sitting outside one of the huts which confirmed the Intel had been correct. Each man carried an AK47 but looked quite relaxed as if they did not expect trouble.

Little did the VC realise, trouble was approaching and *'hell was following close behind'*.

Ski checked his watch. They were now 15 minutes behind schedule but it would not be a problem unless the boat and its cargo arrived early.

During their briefing in Da Nang, they had used a mud map prepared by the LDNN so every man knew the layout of the area and his position in the ambush including their exfil location if they had to making a fighting withdrawal.

The huts were only 30 yards from the river bank so the Team would have all possible exits covered. The VC would be ensnared in a near textbook trap, one from which no one should escape.

Ski gave the thumbs up for the team to move into position. As each man silently moved forward, the LDNN and the SEAL who had been on point, indicated the direction each one needed to take and pointed out the location and number of bad guys.

Once the platoon was in place, Willy and Stan followed Ski to a position from where they could see the Huts without being seen themselves. One SEAL remained near their point of entry to cover their rear. They settled down for the wait.

As part of their brief, each member of the team had been told that when the ambush was initiated, they were only to take down the Vietnamese who carried rifles or were seen by their actions to be a threat.

The intention was to capture alive anyone who was carrying a side-arm as this was normally an indication of an officer. Under interrogation he would be a wealth of potentially important strategic information.

From their concealed positions in the bush, Willy could see that most of the VC were smoking cigarettes and generally very relaxed. He could make out that there were indeed 5 adult males sitting with their backs to the wall of one of the huts and all were facing the river, away from where the SEALs had taken up their ambush positions.

Ski was carefully scanning the area using his Starlight scope, taking note with his experienced eye, the layout of the huts, the total number of weapons and possible escape routes.

Once Ski was satisfied that his Team was in the best positions to effectively carry out the mission, he gave several hand signals to his Chief. Without a word the Chief was gone. Like a ghost fading into the night, to take up his position in the ambush.

The op-plan called for either the Chief or Ski to initiate the ambush. Once it started all hell would break loose. The SEALs were experts in laying down a very accurate and withering rate of fire. The VC wouldn't know what hit them.

Ski's men had worked as a highly structured and tight knit team for their past 4 months in-country so it was accepted without question that the two Aussies not take part in the opening moments of the firestorm but remain in a state of readiness to backup as required. It was agreed that they would keep a watchful eye for anyone trying to escape the ambush.

The total calm of the night was interrupted by the distant sound of a small diesel engine. As they watched and waited, it gradually grew in intensity.

Willy looked sideways at Ski and then at Stan. Ski didn't move a muscle but Willy sensed his increased focus. Stan returned his glance and from that familiar dark face, covered in cam cream, he saw the flash of white teeth.

Willy's immediate thought was, *'The bastard is enjoying this'*. But so was he. He felt his nerves tingling. This was what it was all about. They had a job to do and it sure as hell beat being at home. All their training led to this moment. It came down to their training and talents against the Vietnamese communists' training and talents. It was to be a test of skill.

Willy had no doubt whatsoever that he was on

the winning side.

The boat nudged into the river bank and all the VC had walked down to the shoreline to meet them. The three man boat crew came ashore and they all stood in a huddle while the senior men engaged in hushed conversation. It was the perfect opportunity.

Chief Dalton and another SEAL were positioned between the huts and the riverbank, no more than 20 yards from the cluster of VC. The two of them could easily take out the entire group.

The night erupted in gunfire. Red tracer ripped through the night, tearing into the men. The remainder of the SEAL platoon held their fire. All of the VC went down in the space of two or three seconds. It was a walk in the park.

Complete silence returned to the riverbank. Dalton and his partner stealthily moved forward, weapons at the ready.

The Chief had been selective in his targets and two men were clearly still alive, albeit wounded. They quickly disarmed them and Dalton called out for Ski to come forward. The rest of the platoon didn't move but remained in their positions, ever vigilant, covering their arcs of fire.

Willy and Stan cautiously moved forward with Ski, weapons ready, their eyes searching everywhere. The Vietnamese LDNN materialized out of the shadows and was at their side. He immediately pulled out his K Bar and went straight to one of the VC who was moaning but obviously very much alive. He dragged the man's black trousers to his knees, grasped his genitals in one hand and let loose with a string of clearly threatening Vietnamese. It was obvious that he intended to remove the man's family jewels there and then if he didn't provide the information they wanted.

They later discovered that he had given the man 30 seconds to tell them where the main cache of weapons and ammunition was situated, or his sex life was at a permanent end. It clearly worked. The man wasn't prepared to lose his pride and joy over a cache of weapons. He was terrified and talked rapidly.

The LDNN quickly translated and indicated which hut held the cache. Stan nodded to Willy and said *"You take the boat and I'll look after the hut. Set the fuse and standby for the OK when to pull."*

Willy, with Chief Dalton at his side, headed for the boat with his backpack full of C-4 plastic explosives. The LDNN quickly bound the two wounded VC and began searching the other bodies for documents. Ski and Stan headed straight for the hut supposedly containing the cache.

The boat was loaded with crates of AK47s and boxes of ammunition. While Dalton conducted a quick search of the boat for satchels which might contain money or documents, Willy methodically placed high explosive on the crates and linked it all with detonating cord. Dalton came back to the hold with 2 satchels in his hand and gave the thumbs up.

Willy said *"Ready to go."* The Chief

disappeared through the hatch as Willy attached the safety fuse and blasting cap to the detonating cord trunkline. He then climbed out of the hold to await the signal from Stan.

Meanwhile Stan and Ski had discovered the false floor in one of the huts. They were both taken aback at the quantity of arms stored in what was a large earthen cellar. Fortunately it was very neatly packed, crate upon crate which made it easier to demolish.

Working quickly, Stan rigged his charges and connected it to his detonating cord ringmain. Ski called down that Willy had indicated that he was hooked up and ready to go.

When he was set, Stan said,

"OK ready. We've got 10 minutes from when we pull."
Ski replied,

"Wait one - on my call." He moved to the door and in a voice loud enough for his platoon to hear said,

"On my count of three, we pull and get our asses out of here. We've got ten minute fuses."

"Standby - one, two, three, PULL."

At the same instant, Stan and Willy pulled the pins and each called,

"Fire in the hole."

As Willy came off the boat, Chief Dalton hoisted one of the wounded VC onto his shoulders and they walked to the hut where Stan and Ski waited. Willy glanced at the other VC who had initially survived the ambush but it was obvious he had already passed on to meet his ancestors.

The remainder of the platoon appeared out of

the bushes and after a quick head count, they moved out in single file, led by the LDNN. The radioman was already in contact with the choppers circling somewhere in the distance, passing instructions for their extraction. The LDNN was leading them to a clear area some 500 yards from the huts.

Stan called 5 minutes to go. When he said *"2 minutes."* Ski called a halt and the platoon went to ground utilizing the best cover they could find.

Four seconds after Stan called *"Now"* the night behind them erupted in the first fireball, followed almost immediately by the second. No-one looked back. The bright flash would have destroyed their night vision. Pausing only briefly to listen for any falling shrapnel, Ski called,

"OK, Move out."

Several minutes later they were at the clearing. Without a word from Ski or the Chief, the SEAL platoon immediately set up a defensive perimeter at the edges of the clearing while the radioman called in the choppers.

As time was of the essence, Ski fired a small pocket flare into the sky. Within minutes they heard the reassuring thump of the Hueys inbound. Two of the SEALs moved to both extremities of the clearing and activated two green chemical lights, bright enough for the pilots to see but not so bright that it affected their night vision. The radioman talked them in.

As the first chopper touched down, Dalton with the wounded VC and several of the platoon were scrambling aboard. No sooner had it lifted off and the second one was taking its place on the LZ. The third chopper had barely settled to the ground when the last of the team were aboard and the pilot started pulling on his collective, climbing away under maximum power.

Nobody wanted to spend a second longer than necessary on the ground at night in Charlie country.

Ten minutes later they were touching down on the chopper pad back at Dong Ha. The captured VC was taken away for medical treatment and interrogation and the whole team were led to a building for the debrief.

A sizeable amount of cash and two satchels of documents were handed over to the intelligence staff - a good night's work. The LDNN advised Ski that their captured VC was in fact an NVA (*North Vietnamese Army*) Captain.

As the debrief was being wrapped up, an army Lieutenant stuck his head in the door and advised that there was a Marine CH-46 Sea Knight turning up on the pad which was heading for Da Nang and had room if they wanted a lift. Ski nodded and they filed outside into the early morning sunrise. A long night, but a valuable one.

By the time the chopper was airborne, to a man, they were all sound asleep.

Back in their hooch for a late breakfast, a weary Stan briefed John on the night's events.

When Stan had finished, John said,

"Glad you're both back. Must admit I didn't sleep too

well last night."

And then as if an afterthought he asked,

"What do you think about working with these blokes Stan?"

"I've got no problems Boss. I'd be happy to work with them anytime. They definitely have their shit together." And with his usual shit grin said – *"Just like us."'*

As Stan was heading for a hot shower and his rack, he turned back to Pete and Dusty,

"Forgot to say the SEALs are coming over for a BBQ and a few beers about 1700. Sort it out will you. Lots of steaks and ribs and beans and some of that great Yankee potato salad I like. I know I can count on you blokes."

It was a very relaxed and enjoyable night. The elite of the US Military system, *'frogs'* as they liked to be called, and the Australian Navy's elite *'frogmen'*. They now had each other's measure. None of them were loud or pretentious, just professional sailors who were relaxed and comfortable in each other company. Nothing to prove to each other. In this company, men were judged by their actions and level of competence, not by what they said or alleged to be.

The previous night's op was talked about only briefly and light heartedly and then the conversation moved onto what sailors the world over talked about – beer and women.

CHAPTER 16

Thankfully the few days following the SEAL op were quiet for the Aussie divers. No calls. Willy and Dusty were on stand down the following morning so they launched the skimmer and under the pretext of giving their outboard motor a test run, spent the morning water ski-ing on the harbour.

Dusty was a bit of a barefoot specialist so the motor had a good workout and was deemed to be running well. The weather was perfect and they returned to the hooch with a good dose of sunburn. When Stan saw them, he grinned, *"Tough duty eh?"* Dusty, always being the smart-ass, replied *"Somebody's got to put in the hard yards Chief."*

As they entered the Hooch, Pete casually remarked,
"While you bastards were out cruising around the harbour like a couple of old retired Admirals living it up on a government pension, Matt and I have been hard at work."
Unable to suppress his grin any longer, he continued,
"I've talked the Donut Dollies into coming over tonight for a BBQ. I'm in charge of the booze and organizing the entertainment and you mongrels are doing the cooking."

Willy replied with a chuckle,

"You couldn't organize a short time in a whorehouse if you had a fistful of 100 dollar bills."

Stan was a born cook and he took a lot of pride in his cooking skills. He always took charge of the preparation of the food when they had a special night organized. Even though the rest of the team regularly told him he couldn't boil an egg, he was well aware that they all really enjoyed his cooking.

The Americans flew in tons of frozen steaks from the US and the Aussies had no problems getting all they wanted.

Stan set to work and prepared his favourite potato and bean salads and marinated the steaks with his special homemade BBQ sauce. He was in his element.

While he went to work, the young sailors sat around with a beer and took the piss out of him. Anyone else tried it and he would have had their guts for a necktie, but his boys could get away with it. They were his *'boys'*.

The conversation moved around to the *'Dollies'*. It was obvious to all that a couple of the girls were getting quite attached to these cocky young sailors from *'down under'* and a couple of relationships were under way. Dusty and Willy were becoming the centre of attention and were quite attached to two of the girls.

While he was mixing his special sauce, Stan said with his usual shit eating grin,

"The Dollies aren't the slightest bit interested in you pair of bastards. They only come to the Hooch because of

174

my outstanding cooking."

Pete piped up and said,

"Stan, the girls come here in SPITE of your cooking."

"That's not what they told me. They reckon you're all a pain in the ass – a bunch of wankers. They prefer more mature gentlemen like me."

John poked his head around the corner with a big smile on his face. He also had a handful of mail.

"You blokes aren't still taking the piss out of Stan's cooking are you? You know how sensitive he is, and did I hear someone say 'gentlemen'?? Anyway, I've got some good news and some bad news. What do you want first?"

Pete piped up and said,

"I guess the bad news is that I'm going out on a job tonight while the rest of these bastards cut my grass behind my back with the Donut dollies."

"No, you're safe Pete. I'll give you the good news first just to soften the bad news. The good news is that as of last week, Stan has been promoted to Chief Petty Officer."

John paused and laughed,

"The bad news is Stan is buying the beer tonight."

John then put out his hand.

"I'd like to say on behalf of us all Stan that it is thoroughly deserved and well overdue. Congratulations."

The grinning troops lined up behind John to shake Stan's hand and congratulate him.

"Thanks Boss. Thanks boys. The worst part about it is I have to buy you bastards a beer. What are doing Dusty? Get off your lazy ass and grab some cold beers."

Dusty pouted,

"Damn, he's only been a Chief for 30 seconds and he's givin' me a hard time already."

Stan replied with the biggest grin they had seen in a long time,

"You ain't seen nothing yet. Things are going to change around here. You bastards are going to show some respect from now on... no more takin' the piss out of my cooking."

They all laughed as Dusty passed around cold beers and said, *"You're got to earn our respect Chief, and it doesn't come cheap."*

John raised his can and said,

"Here's to the Chief."

"To the Chief." echoed around the room.

"By the way, I've asked Army EOD downtown to cover for us tonight unless something big comes up. I'll take the duty with Matt so the rest of you can celebrate with the biggest raw bone Chief in the CD Branch."

By the time the Donut Dollies arrived, the boys were well and truly fired up. The girls crowded around to hug Stan and congratulate him. He was in his element.

"See, what did I tell you wankers? These gorgeous young ladies only come here to see me."

The following day it was business as usual. To help shake off the hangovers, the new Chief took the boys for a PT session and a fast 30 minute run around the base. Dusty groaned aloud,

"See what happens when you make Chief in this Navy - get all conscientious and become a pain in the ass."

Stan laughed,

"You pussies need toughening up. You're all behaving like a bunch of sheilas. I've been getting too soft on you lot. About time I made you into real Clearance Divers."

That night no-one felt like a beer and they were all in bed early. It was just as well as the radio crackled into life at 0250 the following morning.

"Cliffside Bravo, this is Cliffside, over."

Stan was out of bed and responding to the call within 10 seconds.

"Cliffside Bravo, go ahead."

"Cliffside Bravo, we have swimmers spotted at the Deep water ammunition piers. We have been advised two confirmed sightings. Request you investigate ASAP, over."

Stan replied,

"Roger Cliffside, on our way, out. Dusty, Pete, Willy, you heard the man, let's go."

Fifteen minutes later their jeep, Willy driving, red light flashing, pulled up at the main entrance to the piers. The young Lt. JG on duty was waiting for them in his Jeep to lead them to the vessel where the swimmers had been spotted.

As they came to a halt on the wharf, Stan was out of the vehicle and listening to a briefing from the officer and the sentries who had spotted the sapper swimmers. The Team gathered around as the sentries explained what they had seen.

Luckily, as the wharf area was very well lit at night, the sentries had spotted a burst of bubbles between the ship's side and the wharf. Several seconds later two Vietnamese divers had briefly broken the surface. Both sentries immediately opened fire with their M16s but were unsure if they hit either one as both divers quickly submerged again.

The senior of the two sentries stated that he thought one of the divers appeared to be in some sort of distress. No more bubbles were observed after they had emptied their magazines into the water. The officer then informed the EOD team that the ship in question was loaded to the gunwales with 500lb and 1000lb bombs and that a skimmer boat was secured at the base of nearby steps for use by the Team.

Stan instructed the officer to clear the wharf ASAP and remove all personnel, including the ship's crew, several hundred meters to the front gate.

"We'll do a quick sweep of the inboard side of this vessel to see if they managed to attach anything to the hull, beginning with where the bubbles were seen. We'll keep you advised by radio Sir, and can you turn on every damn overhead light you have here on the wharf. Let's move it Boys."

If there was a charge on the hull, they all knew that time wasn't on their side. The odds were heavily in favour of the sapper swimmers. This was where they had to hope like hell that if one of the enemy divers was in some sort of distress, the pair didn't have time to attach and arm an explosive device.

Pete volunteered to do the first dive. Visibility wasn't too bad as the wharves were located near the mouth of Da Nang harbour. Pete switched on his powerful underwater torch and began sweeping the beam across the hull in front of him as he descended into the dark and menacing depths. His only contact with the surface, a lifeline secured about his waist which was carefully attended by one of his mates in the boat.

Stan had told him to make a sweep all the way to the keel before heading back to the waterline as their best chance of finding anything was in the area adjacent to where the sappers had been seen on the surface.

Several minutes into the dive, they all heard and felt a sharp short thump through the hull of the skimmer.

Stan said to no-one in particular,

"What the fuck was that? Something went bang."

"Sounded like a thunderflash. Just got a check from Pete. He's OK." Willy reported.

"Roger, he'll be back on the surface shortly so we'll see what the hell that was all about." said Stan.

Thirty seconds later Pete surfaced, pulled his demand valve from his mouth and said,

"You're not going to believe this, but there's a fucking big homemade VC mine tucked under the bilge keel and it just mis-fired while I was checking it out. The detonator functioned but looks like the primer failed. Thank Christ for that. How lucky can you get. It's floating up against the bilge keel with two buoyancy bags. Give me a line and I'll take it down so you can haul the bastard to the surface. Once I've secured it, take the slack and I'll puncture one of the flotation bags."

While Pete went back down to secure a line to

the mine, Stan said to Willy and Dusty,

"Luck of the Irish eh? I reckon we got it sorted. Two divers could only tow one charge so no point looking any further. Goddamn lucky. I wonder what everyone else is doing on this lovely fucking evening while we're up to our asses in alligators."

Willy knew Stan was just talking to ease the tension so he added with a grin,

"I think I need a fucking large Jack Daniels."

"You and me both."

After Pete had secured the line to the mine, it was a relatively simple matter to drag it up to the boat. The three of them then managed to lift it into the skimmer. Once Pete was back inboard, Stan took a long careful look at it and said,

"About 60kgs I reckon. Blasting cap has fired. Definitely primer failure. Would have done a bit of damage. Thank Christ Charlie has to make do with communist made crap. Flash up the motor Willy, I want to do a slow sweep under the wharf. I've got a weird feeling - like someone's watching us."

Willy started the 85 hp Johnson and idled slowly in under the wharf.

Stan said,

"Hand me that aircraft landing light of yours Pete and we'll see if anything is under here. You blokes put one up the spout and keep your eyes peeled. You never know what we might find down here tonight."

They idled the full length of the pier without seeing anything. Stan was not satisfied and told Willy to do a return sweep in the opposite direction.

They were about midway back to their starting point when Dusty pointed and indicated to Stan to swing his torch beam back to where it had just passed. There was a wet patch of timber next to one of the thick vertical footings. They immediately brought their weapons to bear and Willy took the boat around in a slow arc so they could see the other side of the timber pier. Stan's instincts were right on.

There in the light beam appeared a small frightened Vietnamese face staring back at them. He immediately thrust his arms into the air and cried, *"Chieu Hoi, Chieu Hoi."* (meaning I surrender or I defect).

Drawing his .45 handgun, Stan said, *"Cover the little bastard. If he drops his hands, shoot him. Pete, keep your eyes peeled for his mate. Remember they reckon they spotted two of them. OK Willy, let's get closer."*

As they drew nearer, they made out the skinny but wiry little form of the VC swimmer squatting on the crossbeam.

He had obviously ditched his diving set and was only wearing swimming trunks. His wet fins were laying next to him on the beam.

As the skimmer drew alongside, Stan, pointing his weapon at him, indicated that he keep his arms in the clear and jump down into the boat. Pete quickly had him face down on the floor of the boat and began securing his arms and legs behind his back with a divers' lifeline.

Stan picked up the handset of the PRC 25 radio,

"Harbour Security, this is Cliffside 6, we have found and recovered an explosive device from the vessel's hull and captured one, repeat one, Victor Charlie sapper swimmer from under the wharf. Will continue brief search for his buddy and suggest you immediately instigate a thorough boat sweep around the piers. The recovered device is in a safe condition, I say again, safe condition. Returning to wharf landing in 5. Out."

By the time they idled the boat around to the landing, the young officer and two armed sentries were waiting for them.

The VC swimmer was dragged out of the boat and immediately handcuffed by the sentries who then whisked him away in a jeep for interrogation.

Stan briefed the Security officer on the chain of events and the divers loaded up their jeep and wearily headed back to their Hooch. As always, John was up waiting for them. A cup of coffee to settle the nerves and a round-table to update John on the details of the night's operation. As always the paperwork would have to be completed.

The next morning Stan and Willy tracked down the location where the captured VC had been taken for questioning. It was in their interest to find out as much as possible about any information that he had revealed during his interrogation. In particular, they were very interested in his unit's strength, equipment and training.

The VC sapper swimmer had spent a very uncomfortable night being interrogated by ARVN personnel in an empty shipping container located at the Deep water Piers.

The ARVN interpreter informed Stan and Willy that the prisoner was a member of '471 VC Naval Sapper Battalion' which operated in and around Quang Nam Province to the south of Da Nang.

They were taken to see him. He had obviously endured a bad night; both eyes were mere slits, his lips were swollen and his nose didn't look quite straight.

During the course of the interrogation he had volunteered to 'Chieu Hoi'- loosely translated as defecting to the side of the South Vietnamese Government.

The up side for the Aussie divers was at least they now had a name for the enemy sapper unit they were up against. But unfortunately the information had come a little too late.

As their sixth month in country rolled by, news arrived from Australia that the next Team which was on standby to replace them, would not be coming.

The Australian 'withdrawal' from Vietnam had begun.

To a man the news was a bitter pill. They had served their time and had done their best, but they all knew the job was far from completed.

You didn't need to be an Einstein to figure out that the withdrawal was no more or less than a political vote catching decision. The war was unpopular with the voters back home in both the US and Australia. The drug taking protesting pussy brigade had finally gotten their way. The government was taking the easy way out, in essence saying – *'We're taking our ball and going home – we don't want to play anymore!!'*

To a man, they all felt they were betraying the Vietnamese people by leaving with the job unfinished. After a 10 year Australian presence, the door was now being slammed shut.

They all knew the war had not been fought efficiently because of excessive political interference and very ordinary senior military leadership but a complete withdrawal was no less than handing the country to the North Vietnamese communists on a silver platter.

Mama San was particularly upset to hear that the Aussie sailors were going home and that her employment was coming to an abrupt end.

The team dug into their cash slush fund which had been saved from beer sales over their bar and gave her every dollar, although even this failed to cheer her up to any great degree.

She sensed things were only going to go downhill for the South and the team's imminent departure brought that realization to the surface. Fortunately she had agreed to take Dog to her home and look after him but everyone felt very sad about leaving him as they knew life was going to be particularly tough for him.

On the day the team finalized their packing, Dog was quite noticeably agitated. When their truck arrived at Mama San's house on the way to the airport, he was shaking and yelping like a young pup.

The poor old fella knew his *'family'* weren't coming back.

After seven months in South Vietnam, the last Team departed Da Nang aboard a Royal Australian Air Force DHC-4 *'Caribou'* to spend seven days drinking and winding down with their US Navy EOD mates in Saigon.

They visited one of their favourite bars one night to find it partly demolished and in flames. Only minutes before they arrived, two VC had ridden past on a motorcycle and thrown a satchel charge of explosives through the door, killing everyone inside.

Tu Do Street was revisited on a regular basis until finally on the 5th May 1971, they boarded their Qantas *'Freedom Bird'* at Tan Son Nhat airport and headed home to Australia - leaving the rice paddies and mountains of Vietnam behind them forever…...

ABOUT THE AUTHOR

The author spent 20 years as a Clearance Diver in the Royal Australian Navy during the '60s through to the mid '80s, retiring as a Senior Chief Petty Officer and was a member of the 8th and final Clearance Diving Team to serve in South Vietnam.

During his 20 years service, career highlights included;

- Serving in CDT3 in South Vietnam during 1970 & 1971.
- Personnel Exchange Program with the USN from 1977 to 1980 based in Hawaii.
- Obtaining his US Navy Parachute wings at NAS Lakehurst, New Jersey.
- Numerous SPECWAREXs with US Special forces.
- Senior Demolitions Instructor in the RAN and numerous postings to operational diving teams.

After leaving the Navy he was employed by DuPont Explosives as their Specialty Blasting Manager (he developed a specialised *'Shaped Charge'* for DuPont which was patented worldwide) and afterwards had a business in Hanoi, Vietnam, until his retirement in 1997.

His hobbies include international travel, writing, photography, spending time in the

Queensland 'outback' and riding his Harleys in both Queensland and the western United States.

The author holds both US and Australian Pilot licenses with a multi-engine endorsement.

He resides in Redland Bay, Queensland, Australia and has two children - his son is a current serving Clearance Diver in the RAN.

The author in Da Nang - 1970.

GLOSSARY OF TERMS

ARVN – Army of the Republic of South Vietnam.

B&MD - Bomb & Mine Disposal.

CDT - Clearance Diving Team.

CDT3 - CDT3 was formed for *'Special Operations'* in Vietnam. It was disbanded when the 8th and final team was withdrawn from Vietnam in May 1971 and was reformed again for the Gulf War.

Chief Petty Officer – at that time, the highest non-commissioned rank in the RAN - E8 equivalent.

CO - Commanding Officer.

Cooked off – unplanned detonation.

DMZ – The Vietnamese De-militarized Zone ran from east-west near the center of present-day Vietnam (spanning more than a hundred kilometers) and was a couple of kilometers wide. It ran along the Ben Hai River for much of its length. The area within 5 km on either side of the border was declared to be a demilitarized zone. Troops of both governments were barred from this area. It was approximately 62 miles (100 kilometers) north of the city of Hue.

EOD – Explosive Ordnance Disposal.

Freedom Bird – the nickname given to the flight taking you home from Vietnam.

High Order detonation - results in an explosive ordnance producing a designed/intended explosive yield.

Hooch – Accommodation.

Klick – kilometer.

Low Order detonation - a controlled ordnance detonation or a malfunctioned ordnance detonation that results in a significantly lower yield than designed.

NAS – Naval Air Station.

PETN - Penta Erythritol Tetra Nitrate.

Petty Officer - at that time, the 2nd highest non-commissioned rank in the RAN – E7 equivalent.

Rack – Bed.

RAN – Royal Australian Navy.

Saigon – On 2 July 1976, Saigon was officially renamed Ho Chi Minh City by the North Vietnamese victors.

Shaped charge – an explosive charge shaped to focus its explosive energy. Also known as the 'Munroe Effect'.

Short – very close to going home.

SLR – Australian Army issue 7.62mm 'FN' self loading rifle.

SPECWAREX – Special Warfare Exercise.

White Phosphorus (Willy Pete) - burns fiercely and can ignite cloth, fuel, ammunition and other combustibles. Also a highly efficient smoke-producing agent, burning quickly and producing an instant blanket of smoke.

The full version of 'Uc Dai Loi Cheap Charlie':-
(this ditty is sung to the tune of
'Nick Nack Paddywack,
Give the Dog a Bone'.)

"Uc Dai Loi, cheap Charlie,
He no buy me Saigon tea,
Saigon tea cost many many Pi,
Uc Dai Loi, he cheap Charlie.

Uc Dai Loi, cheap Charlie,
He no give me MPC,
MPC costs many many Pi,
Uc Dai Loi he Cheap Charlie.

Uc Dai Loi, cheap Charlie
He no go to bed with me,
Bed with me costs many many Pi
Uc Dai Loi him Cheap Charlie.

Uc Dai Loi, cheap Charlie
Make me give him one for free,
Mamma-San go crook at me,
Uc Dai Loi, he Cheap Charlie.

Uc Dai Loi, cheap Charlie,
He give baby-san to me,
Baby-san costs many many Pi
Uc Dai Loi, he Cheap Charlie.

Uc Dai Loi, cheap Charlie
He go home across the sea,
He leave baby-san with me,
Uc Dai Loi he Cheap Charlie."

Charlie: pronounced char-lee.

Cheap Charlie: a 'round-eye' who was stingy or unwilling to spend money.

Uc-Dai-Loi: is Vietnamese slang for an Australian (pronounced *'ook die loy'*). In Vietnamese, *'Uc'* means Australia.

Saigon Tea: served to bar girls as whisky and coke at inflated prices when a 'round eye' was paying. It was never alcoholic and was usually just cold tea.

MPC: Military Payment Certificates which replaced American dollars. It was an American attempt to get US currency out of the system. MPC was of no use to the NVA or VC and could be changed by the authorities regularly to maintain currency control. All Allied troops had to use it.

Pi: Piastre – the major unit of currency of French Indochina and South Vietnam. MPC was equivalent to about 1,000 Piastre (or more) on the black market. The official Vietnamese currency was, and still is the Dong (VND).

Mamasan: female brothel/bar owner.

Baby San: Baby.

42856858R00110

Made in the USA
Middletown, DE
23 April 2017